# STREET NAMES OF THE CITY OF LIVERPOOL

BY

## STEVEN HORTON

First published 2002 by Countyvise Limited, 14 Appin Road, Birkenhead, Merseyside, CH41 9HH.

Copyright © 2002 Steven Horton.

The right of Steven Horton to be identified as the author of this work has been asserted by him in accordance with the Copyright, Design and Patents Act 1988.

British Library Cataloguing in Publication Data.
A catalogue record for this book is available from the British Library.

ISBN 1 901231 30 5

I would like to express my gratitude to the following:-

All staff at the Liverpool Record Office
Jim Bennett

This book is dedicated to Lynne.
Thank you for all your patience and support.

# FOREWORD

At some stage in a person's life, the question must surely be asked 'How does the street I live in get its name?' This book aims to answer some of your questions, but the fact that developers didn't have to give an explanation when naming streets means that the origins of many names will forever be a secret. Liverpool's size also means it is impossible to give an explanation for every street, but I have attempted to be as comprehensive as can be.

Rather than contain just a brief description of where different streets got their names from, this book aims to show how patterns have changed over time. In doing this I have attempted to portray a historical development over the years as the make up of the city has changed.

The earliest streets tended to be fairly simple. They were lanes or tracks and generally named after where they led or nearby buildings. Of the original seven streets of Liverpool, none were named after people. Many of the old country lanes were not necessarily officially named at all, instead they were simply known as 'the road to the quarry' or 'the road to Everton'.

As development gathered pace in the 18th century, merchants would lay streets through their land and in many cases name them after themselves. During this period, nearly all members of the self-electing Town Council would be honoured. In other cases, streets would be named after Prime Ministers, prominent national politicians or Royal Family members. For instance the length of time spent on the throne by George III is reflected in the amount of streets named after him and his family in the city centre.

In the 19th century more larger scale planned development by private builders occurred. Developers were free to choose their own names and many throughout the city would honour great literary figures such as Charles Dickens and Sir Walter Scott, or remember their Welsh or Scottish homelands and perhaps family members. This trend continued in the 20th century with streets developed by both the local authority and private developers being named after a certain theme. Towns up and down the country were popular, while other examples were golf courses, rivers or flowers. Politicians and royalty are rarely honoured today and this is reflected by the virtual absence of streets related to the family of Queen Elizabeth II and the fact we may never see a Diana Drive, despite the popularity of the late princess.

As we enter the 21st century, it seems increasingly unlikely that we will see a Blair Drive, Harry Close or William Way, while only time will tell if modern day authors such as J.K. Rowling or Stephen King are ever commemorated by streets. Nobody knows what the future holds, but it is certain that new streets will always be required and builders and local authorities will always be coming up with new names.

# CONTENTS

A Plan of LIVERPOOL, AND THE POOL; as they appeared about the Year 1650.

Plan of Liverpool in 1650

Smith - Liverpool Past, Present and Future H942 721 SMI, by courtesy of the Liverpool Record Office

# THE ORIGINAL SEVEN STREETS OF LIVERPOOL

From the time of King John's charter in 1207 until 1650, Liverpool's layout remained essentially the same. Seven streets formed the built up area of the town and these all remain in existence today in more or less their original position, taking their names from local buildings and features.

During this period, Liverpool's skyline was dominated by the castle, which stood on the site of the present Queen Victoria Monument. This was built in the 13th century on what was high-level rock to the west of the Pool, which was a water inlet that ran along the line of present day Paradise Street and Whitechapel. **Castle Street** connected the castle to the built up area of the town.

Juggler Street, which is now called **High Street**, was probably named after the itinerant jugglers that roamed the country practising their art in the centre of towns. The name changed to High Street in the early 18th Century, the name traditionally given to the main trading street of a town. However, the change could also have reflected the fact that the construction of the second Town Hall, which had been completed in 1676, had necessitated the removal of the town's High Cross[1] . With Exchange Flags not then in existence, High Street was much longer than its present form as it connected Castle Street with **Old Hall Street.** This led to the Old Hall, which was built in the 13th century by the Moores family as More Hall. They moved to Bank Hall in Kirkdale in the late 14th century and Old Hall, as it became known, was used as a dower house[2] . This remained a private road until the hall and surrounding lands were sold to the Earls of Derby in 1712, with many wealthy merchants then building properties there.

The three streets mentioned so far are all north to south, but leading eastwards and eventually out of town were **Dale Street** and **Tithebarn Street.** The former led to a dale and was no more than a rough track in those days that connected with the Townsend Bridge, which crossed the Pool. Tithebarn Street was initially known as Moor Street, as in a heath, rather than in relation to the Moore family who were influential in Liverpool at the time. Around 1524, a tithe barn was erected here, although for some time the street was known by both names. A tithe

---

[1] High Cross - place in centre of town where people could meet for religious or other purposes
[2] Dower House - house used as a residence for widow of a deceased male family member

barn was a building that was used to store a tax of the time known as a tithe, whereby 1/10 of produce had to be paid to the clergy. Following the Dissolution of the Monasteries by Henry VIII in 1536 it was owned by Lord Molyneux and used as an ordinary barn.

The final two streets connected the town with the banks of the River Mersey. **Chapel Street** led to the Chapel of St Mary Del Key. This stood on a waterfront site next to the present Church of Our Lady of St. Nicholas and was a chapel of ease to St Mary's, Walton, which was Liverpool's main parish church. After Liverpool became a parish in its own right in 1699, the chapel fell into disuse and was used as a school and a tavern before it was demolished in 1814. Until the 16th century **Water Street** had been known as Bank or Banke Street as it led to the riverbank in the days before a sea wall was built. This was the main approach to the town for anyone who may have arrived by boat.

# THE MOORE AND CROSSE FAMILIES
# LIVERPOOL'S FIRST MERCHANTS

In the late 1600s Edward Moore, owner of the Old Hall was the first to extensively develop Liverpool beyond the original streets. Edward was the son of John Moore, a Parliamentarian who was involved in the condemnation of Charles I to death at the end of the Civil War and was the earliest known Liverpool man to trade with the West Indies. Edward carried on this tradition and erected a house off Dale Street in the 1660s for the drying and boiling of sugar, which he imported from Barbados. For centuries, his family had owned most of the land between Castle Street, Old Hall Street and the River Mersey and Edward began the process of developing this, with many of the newly built streets remaining in existence today.

A street laid out linking the castle and river was **Moor Street,** named by Edward after himself and still in existence today in a shorter form. Adjoining this is **Fenwick Street,** which is named after his wife, Dorothy Fenwick. Another street was laid out at Edward's suggestion along a croft[3] between Dale Street and Tithebarn Street owned by John Hackins. This became known as **Hackins Hey,** Hey being a derivation of the French word 'haie', meaning land enclosed by hedges. Hey thus became a common term used in Liverpool to describe small lanes such as this one and **Lancelot's Hey**, which has now been virtually swamped by the Royal/Sun Alliance building, remembers Thomas Lancelot, a lessee of the Moore family. Related to the Moores were the Hockenhalls of Tranmere. One member, Thomas, was a 17th century mayor of Liverpool and they gave their name to **Hockenhall Alley,** off Dale Street.

Edward later became alarmed by erosion of some of his land and the subsequent loss of rent revenue, so suggested a sea wall to arrest this problem. This went on to be built by his son, Cleave Moore and was named **New Quay.** Cleave Moore did not share his father's passion for foreign trade however and went on to lose a lot of the family estates, selling many to the Stanleys, who were Earls of Derby. In the early 1700s, he did develop some streets off Old Hall Street, some of which were named after his family and are still there. **Edmund Street** was laid out to celebrate his marriage and named after his father-in-law, Joseph

---

[3] Croft - small piece of arable land fenced in on all four sides

Edmund. **Union Street** formed a cross roads with this and Old Hall Street and may also have been named after the marriage union, although there is no conclusive evidence of this. There is a possibility it may have been to honour the 1707 Act of Union, which joined together England and Scotland, but due to its proximity to Edmund Street I would suggest that the Moore's marriage influence is more likely.

As well as naming streets after members of their family, some of their tenants were commemorated as well. William Bushell rented land near Castle Street on which he had a rope making business and the street where this stood is now called **Old Ropery.** A shipwright called Roger James, a tenant of the family who lived in Moor Street, may have given his name to **James Street,** although there is no evidence to suggest this. He was one of the few people, however, of whom Edward Moore spoke well.

To the north of Liverpool city centre, **Bankhall Lane** once led to Bank Hall, which became the Moores' principal family residence in the 14th century. Bank Hall remained a home of the Moores family for 400 years before being sold to the Earl of Derby. It was eventually demolished in 1772 and a farmhouse built on the site. **Bankhall Street** also takes its name from this.

Along with the Moores, the Crosse family were major landholders in 17th century Liverpool. The family were involved in one of Liverpool's first ventures into overseas trade when Christopher Crosse began importing Spanish iron from Bilbao in the 16th century. The family lived in Crosse Hall, which stood on the site of the present Municipal Buildings in Dale Street. Centuries old, this was demolished in 1750 to make way for courts[4] and gave its name to the adjoining **Crosshall Street.** When the Blue Coat School vacated its old premises due to their limited size and moved to the nearby Blue Coat Chambers in 1717, John Crosse formed a grammar school on the old site. The road leading to this then became known as **School Lane.** In the early 1800s a new road was built to link Tithebarn Street to Byrom Street and Scotland Road. It was named **Great Crosshall Street** after an ancient windmill belonging to the family that stood near to its junction with Johnson Street, the prefix being added to avoid any confusion with Crosshall Street.

---

[4] Courts - slum properties consisting of a central courtyard surrounded by 2-4 storey dwellings on all sides

4

# THE STANLEYS - THE EARLS OF DERBY

The Stanleys have been influential in the Liverpool area since marrying into the Lathom family of Lathom Hall, near Ormskirk, in the 14th century. After Henry VII became King of England following the Battle of Bosworth in 1485, their support was rewarded with the title Earls of Derby.

In the English Civil War (1642-48), the 7th Earl was executed for his support of the King, Lathom Hall was destroyed and their lands confiscated. After regaining their lands following the restoration of the monarchy in 1660, Knowsley Hall became the main residence and a combination of marriages and purchases saw them become major landowners in the Liverpool area.

The 14th Earl, Edward Geoffrey Stanley, was Prime Minister three times between 1852 and 1868, while his son Edward served him as Foreign Secretary in his final term. Edward later served Gladstone as Colonial Secretary before going on to lead the Liberals in the House of Lords. The family is still going strong and the current earl is Edward Stanley. The family's history and influence locally can be seen in the number of streets named after them across the city.

After buying land from Cleave Moore in the early 18th century the Stanleys laid out **Stanley Street** around 1740. They also formed **Derby Square** on the site of Liverpool Castle, which remained undeveloped until the 1760s despite being levelled and having its ditch filled in some forty years earlier. Before these streets were built however, the family did have a presence in the town for many centuries through their ownership of Liverpool Tower, their seaside residence at the bottom of Water Street. This would also be used as a stopping off point on their visits to the Isle of Man in their capacity as Lords of Man. The Tower disappeared around 1821, having been used as a gaol, school and tavern, but its name is remembered by **Tower Garden,** which ran to the east of it.

In the mid 19th century, some 150 years after lands around Bank Hall were acquired from the Moores, the Stanleys laid out two major roads linking Liverpool and Bootle, where they also owned land. These were

**Derby Road** and **Stanley Road.** Rake Lane, which adjoined Stanley Road, was re-named **Latham Street** after their one-time residence. **William Moult Street** was developed and named after one of the family's land agents in the area, whilst in Everton a steward of the Earls gave his name to the street where he lived, **Carver Street.**

Also in the 19th century, the family sold a large part of the 95 acres of land that would become Stanley Park to Liverpool Corporation. Roads near to this that were named in their honour were **Stanley Park Avenue North** and **Stanley Park Avenue South**. The latter was initially plain Stanley Park Avenue but the suffixes were added in the 1930s when Stanley Park Avenue North was developed.

All streets mentioned so far are in the city centre or north end of Liverpool, but southern areas are not neglected by the Stanley name. **Stanley Street** lies off Prescot Road in an area named after them. There is also a **Derby Street** and **Stanley Street** in Garston, while in Grassendale, **Knowsley Road** is named after their main residence.

# THE EARLS OF SEFTON

The Molyneux family were major landowners in Liverpool from Plantaganet times. In 1446 Henry VI granted Richard Molyneux Croxteth and Toxteth Parks, with Croxteth Hall being built as the family's main residence in 1575. The family were made Earls of Sefton in 1771 but in 1974 Croxteth Hall and Country Park were left to Liverpool City Council after the last earl had died. Their influence in street names can be seen all over the city, but nowhere more so than in Toxteth.

Between 1446 and 1672 the family were the King's representatives in Liverpool and as such leased the Castle. In the mid to late 17th century **Lord Street** was laid out to connect it with a bridge across the Pool, as on the other side of this was their land at Toxteth Park. This was then mainly rural and used for hunting.

In the late 18th century, as Liverpool became more overcrowded, it was decided to build a new town to the south on the land owned by the Earl of Sefton. Following an Act of Parliament in 1775, building leases could be granted for the land and the boundary between Liverpool and Toxteth Park was re-named **Parliament Street** from its original name of Towns End Lane. The town was only meant to extend as far as Northumberland Street and many of these earliest streets, which were laid out in a grid pattern, were named in honour of the Molyneux family.

The original idea was to call the new town Harrington, but the new name never really caught on and the area continued to be known as Toxteth. The intended name was in honour of Isabella, 1st Countess of Sefton, who was daughter of the Earl of Harrington. However, she is still commemorated by **Upper Harrington Street, Stanhope Street** (named after her family surname) and **Upper Stanhope Street.** A relative of hers, Philip Dormer Stanhope, 4th Earl of Chesterfield is remembered by **Chesterfield Street.** Initially there was a Harrington Street, but this was changed to **Caryl Street** after the absorption of Toxteth into Liverpool to avoid confusion with Harrington Street in the city centre. This new name was after Caryl Molyneux, who was the leader of the Royalist troops that ended Prince Rupert's siege of Liverpool during the Civil War.

The Earl of Sefton was himself remembered in **Sefton Street,** while a name change in the late 19th century saw Bedford Street become **Beaufort Street.** This was named after the Duke of Beaufort who acted as guardian to Charles William Molyneux, the first Earl, after he became orphaned at the age of eight in 1756. The Beaufort's seat is Badminton House in Avon, which is remembered in **Badminton Street.**

A street that had been present before the development of Toxteth began was **Lodge Lane,** which led to a shooting lodge of the Earls of Sefton. This is now called Park Lodge and still stands at the bottom of **Sefton Park Road,** which was named when Sefton Park was opened in 1872. This was developed on 387 acres of land that were purchased from the Earl of Sefton by Liverpool Corporation.

Within Sefton Park, **Croxteth Drive** remembers the family's main residence, while **Lathbury Lane** is name after John Lathbury, who was a land agent for the Earl of Sefton and lived at Toxteth Farm, to which the lane once led. Nearby there is also a **Croxteth Road**, which dissects Sefton Park Road, as well as a **Croxteth Grove**.

In other parts of the city, there are a number of streets named Sefton in their honour, such as **Sefton Road** in Walton. The Townsend family leased property from the Molyneux family and gave their name to **Townsend Lane,** which was in existence in 1760, as well as **Townsend Avenue.**

**Croxteth Hall Lane** has led to their ancestral home for hundreds of years and off this is the fairly recently developed **Countess Park,** which has been named after the last Countess of Sefton who died in 1980. Features of a country estate are present in some of the roads built in other new housing developments nearby, such as **Coachmans Drive** and **Huntsman Wood.** Another house belonging to the family was the New Hall, situated near the junction of Muirhead Avenue and Queens Drive. This was demolished to make way for development in 1926, but gave its name to **New Hall Lane.**

# THE SLAVE TRADERS OF LIVERPOOL

Liverpool's role in the slave trade during the 18th century cannot be ignored. The triangular trade involved the shipping of Lancashire produced goods such as cloth to Africa, which were traded for slaves. They were then transported to America and traded for sugar and tobacco before the ships returned to Liverpool. Given the diversity of products involved within the trade, nearly all merchants in Liverpool during this period were involved in some way. This chapter only intends to deal with those who were linked more prominently than others, but the distance between some of the streets concerned demonstrates how many people were involved.

Britain's largest Caribbean colony was Jamaica, where many local merchants had estates. These estates were a major source of sugar and a destination for many slave ships and **Jamaica Street**, near to the docks, was developed in the second half of the 18th century in recognition of this. Around the same time and in the same vicinity **Norfolk Street** was laid out, named after a port in Virginia that played an important part in the shipping of goods from the plantations. **Goree**, which is the northbound carriageway of the main road by the Cunard Buildings, is named after an island off Senegal where slaves would gather for shipment to the plantations. British forces had captured this island from the French in 1759.

One of Liverpool's main shopping streets is **Bold Street**, which is named after a family who owned land at the top of the street, where the bombed out St. Luke's Church stands today. One member of the family was Jonas Bold, who was listed as an African merchant in 1750. In addition to Bold Street, there is also a **Bold Place** and **Back Bold Street**. Another street linked to slavery in the pedestrian shopping area is **Tarleton Street**, named after the Tarleton family who were slave merchants over three generations from the 1720s. Tom Tarleton, 'The Great T', established the family as leading figures, following in his father's footsteps as a slave merchant. He left a reputed fortune of £80,000 and three of his sons went into partnership with Daniel Backhouse, creating the firm Tarleton and Backhouse. By the 1780s they were reputed to be supplying 3,000 slaves a year to the Spanish colonists. The Tarletons are also responsible for the name of **Redcross**

**Street**, which forms the entrance to a car park at the rear of the Queen Elizabeth II Law Courts. This is named after a red stone obelisk that they erected nearby.

Off Hope Street lies **Blackburne Place**. This was named after John Blackburne, a slave merchant who lived there in the 1780s. Back then, this area was in the country and such a desirable residence could only be afforded by the very wealthy, which he had become from the trade. His house, Blackburne House still stands and is now an exhibition and conference centre. Blackburne was originally from Orford, near Warrington, which he remembered with **Great Orford Street**, off Mount Pleasant. He also engaged in the salt trade and his refinery was situated near to Salthouse Dock, which is situated opposite Canning Place and has given its name to **Salthouse Quay**. In 1798 he moved his salt refinery to Garston, where his name is also remembered in **Blackburne Street**.

One of the streets running between Brownlow Hill and Pembroke Place is **Great Newton Street**, named after John Newton (1725-1807). As Vicar of Olney, he co-wrote the Olney Hymns, of which *Amazing Grace* is the best known. Despite eventually campaigning for the abolition of the slave trade, he was captain of a slave ship between 1750-4 while studying for the ministry in Liverpool. This ship was called the African and was owned by Joseph Manesty, who was the town's bailiff in 1757 and lived in **Manesty's Lane**, off Hanover Street. Near the corner of Renshaw Street and Hardman Street is **Oldham Street**, along with **Oldham Place**. These are named after Captain James Oldham, who was engaged in the Africa to West Indies section of the triangle and built the first house in the street. He died at sea in 1825.

Sir Thomas Johnson, who is covered in more detail under 'Merchants and Mayors', gave his name to **Sir Thomas Street**. He was a joint financier of the second recorded slave ship to leave Liverpool, The Blessing, in October 1700. His son-in-law was Richard Gildart, who was Mayor in 1714, 1731 and 1736 and lived until the age of 99. He had been associated with transporting Jacobite rebels[5] to America in 1716 and then came to prominence in the slave trade. His son and grandson, both called James, were also Mayors of Liverpool. **Gildart Street**, off London Road, is named in the family's honour, while nearby **Norton**

---

[5]Name given to supporters of the House of Stuart whose last king, James II, was de-throned by William of Orange.

**Street** takes its name from Norton Hall, a residence of theirs that stood on the street's corner with Islington. The family also gave their name to **Gildarts Gardens** in Vauxhall.

Another three times Mayor and associate of Sir Thomas Johnson was Foster Cunliffe, who is commemorated in the city's business district by **Cunliffe Street**. He leased a house from Johnson and from 1750 was involved in the trade, owning an estate at Chesapeake Bay where slaves worked. His firm, Foster Cunliffe and Sons owned or had a share in four vessels, which were regularly used for slave trading.

In the 1750s John Ashton, who owned the salt works at Dungeon, near Speke, went into the slave trade and in turn invested the profits into the Sankey Canal. His son, Nicholas, purchased Woolton Hall (which still stands today) in 1772 and is remembered in the neighbourhood by **Ashton Square**, as well as **Ashton Drive** in nearby Hunts Cross. The family is also commemorated in the city centre, where there is an **Ashton Street** off Brownlow Hill. Not far from this is **Little Woolton Street**, which was named after the family home.

As well as selling estates to the Stanleys, Cleave Moore sold some of his land around Old Hall Street to the Earle family, who laid out **Earle Street** there. John Earle, an ironmonger served on the Town Council and went into slavery after 1750. His two sons, Ralph and Thomas, both became Mayors and continued the family's involvement in the trade, with Thomas acquiring land outside the city centre known as the Spekelands Estate. This was situated between the current Smithdown Road and Tunnel Road and on it he built a house called Spekelands in 1803, living there until he died in 1822. This land was then built upon around 1870 and **Earle Road** and **Spekelands Road** were named in the family's honour. **Woodcroft Road** was named after a house of the same name that stood on the estate.

In the north of the city two different slave traders, John Atherton and Thomas Leyland, had ownership of Walton Hall. Leyland acquired the property, which stood on the site of the boating lake in Walton Hall Park, from Atherton in 1804. Leyland first accumulated his wealth in a lottery win in 1776, but went on to invest it in ships that were used for privateering and slave trading. The hall was demolished in the early 20th century but is still remembered by **Walton Hall Avenue**, which was opened by George V in 1934.

# LIVERPOOL'S SLAVERY ABOLITIONISTS

While many merchants undoubtedly made a healthy living from slavery, Liverpool still had its abolitionists who did everything they could to have the trade stopped. The Society for the Abolition of the Slave Trade was formed in London in 1787 and soon followed by the Liverpool Committee for the Abolition of the Slave Trade. Slavery was finally outlawed in 1807.

Perhaps the most famous of the local abolitionists was William Roscoe. A self-taught man, he was a lawyer, banker, author and poet, as well as MP for Liverpool. He spoke against the trade in Parliament and was known as someone who may bring down the town because of his views. Despite this he was held in great honour and **Roscoe Street** was named after him some 35 years before his death in 1831. Another street named in his honour is **Roscoe Lane**, which links Roscoe Street with Berry Street. He was buried in the grounds of the Renshaw Street Unitarian Chapel which is now occupied by a bar and restaurant complex. The site of the burial grounds remains however under the name of **Roscoe Memorial Gardens**.

One of Roscoe's homes was a house called Birchfield, situated at the corner of the present day Islington and Canterbury Street. As this area became more built up, he left for Allerton Hall, but **Birchfield Street** commemorates the house that stood until the end of the 19th century. Another home of Roscoe's was a cottage called Bentley, which is remembered by **Bentley Road** in Toxteth. His sister Margaret married Daniel Daulby from Westmoreland, who owned land adjoining Pembroke Place and **Daulby Street** cut through it. The couple took up residence there after they were wed.

In 1696 William Rathbone II arrived in Liverpool where he established a timber business, which was developed along with an international merchanting concern by his son, William Rathbone III (1726-89). He was a committed opponent of the slave trade as was his son William Rathbone IV (1757-1809), who was a founder member of the abolition movement in Liverpool. The Greenbank Estate near Sefton Park, leased in 1788 as a country retreat, gives its name to **Greenbank Lane**, **Greenbank Drive** and **Greenbank Road**. In Wavertree the family are commemorated by **Rathbone Road** while off this is **Binns Road**, named after Dr. Jonathan Binns (1747-1818), a Liverpool medicine man who was a co-founder of the committee.

# THE LONDON INFLUENCE

In the 18th century, it became fashionable up and down the country to name streets and districts after areas of London. Liverpool, which was well on its way to becoming a major international city, was no exception to this and a number of old lanes that were developed were renamed after London streets or districts.

**London Road** was once part of the 'road to Prescot', the main road out of Liverpool. This led all the way to Warrington, but was in such poor condition in the early 18th century that it had to be traversed on horseback. In 1760 it was widened and repaired, meaning that it was now possible to take carriages from Liverpool to all parts of the country, instead of having to pick one up at Warrington. The first coaches from Liverpool to London used to leave from Dale Street and the old road was formally named London Road.

Another route out of Liverpool in the 18th century was Pinfold Lane, which led north towards Bank Hall and Bootle. That was named after a pinfold, a pound for stray animals that was situated near the tithe barn. By 1810 this lane had been renamed **Vauxhall Road**, after a house that was built there and named after Vauxhall Gardens in the London district of Lambeth.

One of the earliest lanes of Liverpool was Dig Lane, which connected Tithebarn Street and Dale Street on the outer fringes of town. This was re-named **Cheapside** by 1725, after an area of the City of London that derived from the old English word for market. A new street northwards was **Pall Mall**, which had begun to be developed by 1765 and takes its London origins from a version of croquet that was played in the late 17th century. **Whitechapel** was re-named after the east London district in the 1770s, having originally been called Frogg Lane due to the fact that the area was a breeding ground for frogs. Whitechapel in London was named after the parish Church of St Mary, which dates from the 13th century.

Liverpool's first purpose built theatre was constructed in 1749, replacing an earlier venue named the Old Ropery that became unsuitable as it had no boxes or gallery. The new theatre was situated near Water Street and the road fronting it was named **Drury Lane**, after the famous London theatre. It remained in use until 1772 when another one was built in Williamson Square. After this it went into decline and was used as a warehouse and fire engine shed until its demolition under the 1786 Improvement Act.[6] Drury Lane in London took its name from a local businessman.

Several University of Liverpool buildings are located on **Oxford Street**, although this is not named after the famous educational institution. This street was laid out at the beginning of the 19th century and named after the street of the same name in London, nearly 100 years before Liverpool's university was founded. On the waterfront and initially laid out in the late 18th century as Wapping Quay, **Wapping** takes its name from a district of the London docklands.

The Ranelagh tea gardens stood from 1722-90 on the site of the Adelphi Hotel. This name was copied from gardens in the house of Lord Ranelagh in the London district of Chelsea. **Ranelagh Street**, which led to the Liverpool tea gardens, was in existence by 1766. Also in existence by 1766 was nearby **Fleet Street**, the London version having been named after a river of the same name that now flows underground. **Newington**, which runs between Bold Street and Renshaw Street, was developed and in existence by 1785 and is named after a district of south London, literally meaning 'new town'.

The old rural lane leading to West Derby was called Folly Lane, after a building of 6-8 storeys called 'The Folly' that stood near to the Wellington Monument. A fair known as Folly Fair used to take place in the fields adjoining it every Easter, which had a reputation for drunkenness and fighting. Around 1780 the folly had been purchased and a house built on its site by Philip Christian. As local fields were swamped by development at the turn of the 19th century, the new main road was re-named **Islington**. This district of north London was mentioned in the Domesday Book but the origins of its name is uncertain.

Off Islington is **Soho Street**, named after a district of west London that was once a hunting ground attached to Westminster Palace. The name So-ho came from a hunting call used to call in the hounds. Two other

---

[6] Act that allowed for the widening of streets and slum clearance.

rural lanes were re-named around the same time as Islington, both after districts of west London. A previously unnamed continuation of Brownlow Hill was named **Paddington**, which in London was named after an Anglo Saxon chief called Padda, while part of the turnpike[7] road to Prescot, Prescot Lane, was re-named **Kensington**. Like Islington, Kensington gets a mention in the Domesday Book, although there is no clear explanation of its name.

---

7 Toll road

# MERCHANTS AND MAYORS OF THE 18TH AND EARLY 19TH CENTURIES

During the 18th century Liverpool grew at an astounding pace, the population rising several fold. During this time the Town Council consisted mainly of merchants and was self-elected. Once on it, a member would sit for life, with two bailiffs[8] and a Mayor being appointed on an annual basis. Many of these merchants and their activities are reflected in the street names in the city centre and hardly a Mayor of Liverpool during this period did not have a street named after him. However many have since disappeared due to redevelopment.

Some of Liverpool's earliest Mayors are commemorated in the area around Dale Street, Tithebarn Street and Old Hall Street. **Fazakerley Street**, for example, was in existence in the early 18th century as Rosemary Lane, but had its name changed by 1785. The Fazakerley family of Walton owned the land here and one member, Roger, was Mayor in 1531, with Samuel Fazakerley later serving as Town Clerk[9] from 1664 to 1668. Off Fazakerley Street, **Spellow Place** commemorates one of their mansions. Two members of the Brooks family, Gilbert and Egidius, were Mayor in 1592 and 1601 respectively. They were from a long established family that is commemorated by **Brook Street**.

**Bixteth Street** and **Sweeting Street** are named after two Mayors from the turn of the 18th century, Alderman Thomas Bickerstath (1701) and Alderman Sweeting (1698). Bixteth Street, where Thomas lived, was laid out in the early 1700s as Bickersteth Street but this was corrupted to Bixteth by 1765, while Sweeting Street was originally known as Elbow Lane due to its shape. Opposite Bixteth Street is **Tempest Hey**, which was developed in the early 1700s and named after the Plumbe Tempest family of Plumbe Hall in Wavertree.

**Rigby Street** was in existence by 1785 and named after Gilbert Rigby who had been Mayor in 1774 and lived on the streets corner with Old Hall Street. Leather was one of the products traded by the merchants and one of the few remaining narrow alleys of Liverpool is **Leather Lane** off Dale Street. Leather skins were sold there in the 18th century.

---

[8] Officer who would enforce municipal orders.
[9] Person who carries out administrative functions of the council.

A cockpit, which was a circular pit dug into the ground once existed in what is now **Cockspur Street**. Cock fighting, which originated in ancient Persia, Greece and Rome, was a fairly gruesome form of entertainment for the merchants. The 'sport' was not outlawed in England until 1849.

At the Vauxhall Road end of Tithebarn Street is **Pownall Square**. This is named after William Pownall, who was Mayor in 1767 but died in office, catching a chill while trying to quell a riot at Devils Acre, near Salthouse Dock. Pownall lived on the corner of Liver Street and **Pownall Street**, which had been named when he was still alive and is situated off Park Lane. This street was originally much longer than it is now, part of it having become **Upper Pownall Street** around 1900. His home village of Tabley in Cheshire was commemorated by **Tabley Street**, which was laid out through land that he owned near his property.

On the opposite side of Park Lane to Pownall Street is **Cleveland Square**, named after John Cleveland who was Mayor in 1703 and later MP between 1710 and 1713. Cleveland owned the land on which **Price Street** was laid, naming it after a branch of his extended family. Nearby there once existed a Bird Street, which was absorbed into Strand Street in the late 18th century. This was named after Alderman Bird, who lived in the street and was Mayor in 1746, but he was not to be forgotten and **New Bird Street**, off Jamaica Street was named in his honour instead.

**Blundell Street** is named after the Blundell family. Bryan Blundell (1676-1756) had an interest in the slave ship Mulberry, but his main concern was as a tobacco merchant. He was twice Mayor of Liverpool and founded the Blue Coat School, an interest his two sons, Richard and Jonathan, retained for forty years after his death. The Blue Coat still exists today in Wavertree, although the old school building remains in use as an art gallery and is the oldest building in Liverpool city centre. Its educational link is reflected by the name of the street on which it stands, **College Lane**. This was originally called Workhouse Lane after a workhouse that stood on Hanover Street between 1732 and 1795.

Peter Rainford, who was bailiff in 1724 laid out a market garden which became known as **Rainford Gardens** and **Rainford Square**, both of which were in existence by 1765 and can be found between Lord Street and Stanley Street. Another square laid out was **Williamson Square**, developed as an exclusive neighbourhood in the 1760s by the Williamson family, who were shoemakers that invested in overseas trade. William Williamson was Mayor in 1761 and shortly after Williamson Square was completed, nearby **Williamson Street** was developed. An unnamed road led from Williamson Square to Limekiln Lane (now Lime Street), then on the outskirts of town. This was later named **Roe Street**, after merchant William Roe who lived in Queen Square in a house that became the Stork Hotel, which was not demolished until the 1970s. **Richmond Street**, connecting Whitechapel with Williamson Square, was named after the Mayor of 1672, Silvester Richmond.

Before 1750, open countryside surrounded the area that is now **Clayton Square** shopping centre. The leaseholder of the land was Sarah Clayton (1712-79), the daughter of colliery owner William Clayton who was MP from 1698 to 1714 and had been Mayor of Liverpool in 1689. Sarah Clayton laid out a square and adjoining streets on the land. The square's size was halved in 1922 when the Owen Owen store (now Tesco) was built. Even further development took place in the 1980s when the shopping mall was built but the original name has survived. The surrounding streets laid out by Clayton are all still there, although some have shortened in length over the years due to building work. **Leigh Street** is named after her mother, Elizabeth Leigh, while three other streets are named after the husbands of her sisters. They are **Cases Street**, **Houghton Street** and **Parker Street**.

Henry Trafford, who had played a part in the construction of Liverpool's first dock, was Mayor in 1740 but died in office. Trafford's Weint was named after him and later became Trafford Street, but from the 1820s this was merged with a street called Love Lane to form what is now **South John Street**. Nearby is **Dorans Lane**, which links Lord Street and Cavern Walks. This was named after an Irish merchant called Felix Doran who lived in Lord Street.

Near the corner of Hanover Street and School Lane is **Brooks Alley**, which was named after a merchant called Joseph Brooks who owned the garden through which it was laid. On the other side of Hanover Street, George Campbell was a sugar boiler and merchant, who was Mayor in

1763 and owned premises on Duke Street. There he dealt in sugar produced by slaves in the West Indies and **Campbell Street** was named after him. Further up Duke Street, Richard Kent, a merchant and ship owner built himself a house in 1768. He then laid out a street adjoining this and named it **Kent Street**. Other streets were developed in this area and named by him in relation to southern counties like his surname. They are **Suffolk Street** and **Surrey Street**. The fact that this district was a fashionable place to live for merchants in the 18th century has been recognised by the recent naming of **Merchants Square**, near Kent Street, as part of a wider re-generation of an area that is now known as the 'Rope Walks'.

Thomas Seel was a merchant who lived in Hanover Street and **Seel Street** was laid out through his gardens at the end of the 18th century. Parallel to this is **Parr Street**, named after a banker called Thomas Parr who lived in **Colquitt Street**, which is named after the Colquitts who owned the land through which it was laid. One of the family members, John was listed in Gores Directory[10] of 1766 as the port's customs collector. Seel Street and Parr Street are both long streets that were developed on the site of old ropewalks, which were needed in the town due to Liverpool's status as a port. The rope walk method of rope making meant that areas with long straight sites were needed, as a machine would simply move slowly on rails twisting the fibres into strands of rope. As Liverpool grew rope making moved further afield to Toxteth, off Lodge Lane and this can be seen by the long nature of the streets there, as many fields used for rope making were then converted into streets quite easily. Another example of an old ropewalk in the city centre is **Renshaw Street**, which was named after its 18th century owner, John Renshaw.

It is a common misconception that **Hope Street** is so called as it connects Liverpool's two cathedrals. The street was in fact there for 150 years before building work commenced on the Anglican Cathedral. It was named after William Hope, a merchant who built the first house in the street on the site of the Philharmonic Hotel. Off Hope Street is **Maryland Street**, which was developed by a tobacco merchant named Mr Hunter. He lived in Mount Pleasant and this street, along with **Baltimore Street** and **South Hunter Street** were laid out in the gardens of his home. Maryland and Baltimore Streets were named after the

---

[10] First published in 1766, an annual directory of streets and principal inhabitants in Liverpool.

location of the plantations and port from which the goods were shipped, while South Hunter Street was so named as a Hunter Street already existed in the north of the city.

**Faulkner Street** and **Falkner Square** remember Edward Faulkner, who was a late 18th century merchant and High Sheriff[11] of Lancashire. The differing spellings may have been caused by sign-writers not being aware of the exact spelling. During his time as High Sheriff, he raised 1,000 local men when a French invasion threatened in 1797. He also built Fairfield Hall to the east of the town, which gave its name to the surrounding district and subsequently **Fairfield Street**.

The merchants of Liverpool needed somewhere known as an exchange to conduct their business as their quarters at the top of Castle Street became too congested. In 1808 an area adjacent to the current Town Hall was purposely developed and named **Exchange Flags**, its name coming from the flagstones that covered the square. **Exchange Passage East** and **Exchange Passage West** were developed as alleys to connect it with the main street networks, while nearby there is an **Exchange Street East**. This is because the exchange was once situated in the Town Hall itself, prior to 1755. Merchants also had to pay duties on imported goods and a new Custom House was built next to the Old Dock in 1722, replacing the one that had stood at the bottom of Water Street. **Custom House Lane** led to the new building, which was later replaced by a much grander effort that was destroyed by bombing during the Second World War.

Two men who owned land between Brownlow Hill and Pembroke Place around 1800 and had streets named after them were a Mr Dansey and Mr Gill, who gave their names to **Dansie Street** and **Gill Street**. These streets are near to **Brownlow Hill** and **Brownlow Street**, which are named after Lawrence Brownlow who also owned a lot of land in this vicinity. Running uphill from Lime Street is **Copperas Hill**, which is named after some copperas works that were owned by Richard Hughes, Mayor in 1756. Copperas is an old name for ferrous sulphate, which was used in the manufacture of old inks.

Liverpool had a thriving pottery industry in the 18th century and one potter who built a house on the corner of **Christian Street** and Islington

---

[11] King's chief representative of the country.

was Philip Christian. This street is now much shorter than it originally was due to the Churchill Way flyovers. Perhaps the most famous of all the Liverpool potteries was the Herculaneum Pottery Company in Toxteth. This was in existence from 1796 to 1833 before they were forced to fold due to the level of competition from Staffordshire. The business was carried on by a successor before the site was sold in 1841 and Herculaneum Dock established, which has subsequently led to the naming of **Herculaneum Court** and **Herculaneum Road**.

A civic leader who is not remembered by his surname is Pudsey Dawson, a merchant and ship owner who was Mayor in 1799. He regularly used to give talks at the Atheneum Club when taking snuff and is remembered by his first name in **Pudsey Street**, as Dawson Street was already in existence. Linking Pudsey Street to Lime Street is **Coal Street**, which was the site of a market for Prescot Coal. **Lime Street** takes its name from limekilns[12] that once stood on the site of Lime Street station. It had been known as Limekiln Lane in the mid 18th century, but due to the expanding population the kilns were moved around the turn of the 19th century to the North Shore, where Princes and Waterloo Docks are today. A proprietor of the North Shore limekilns was commemorated in **Chadwick Street**, while in Vauxhall **Limekiln Lane** was named after limekilns were established there. Prior to the onset of limekilns and expansion of the dock system, this area had been a popular bathing resort. A popular inn was owned by a Dutchman named Vandries, who gave his name to **Vandries Street**, while **Bath Street** was named after the seawater baths that had to make way for the construction of Princes Dock in 1817.

With so much development in Liverpool going on at this time, building workers were at a premium and there were profits to be made. In the late 18th century two brothers named Johnson came to Liverpool and set up a building business, naming the street on which it was developed **Johnson Street**, where they also owned adjoining land. They later purchased some more land to build some lime works and named this **Hatton Garden**, after their home village, which is near Warrington. Near to these streets is **Pickop Street**, which was named after the Miles and Pickop brewery that existed there 200 years ago. Responsible for the repair of Liverpool's streets at this time was George Byrom, a

---

[12] Used to produce lime from stone.

builder and pavior who had his yard in Hunter Street. **Byrom Street** takes its name from him, although it was originally known as Dog Kennel Lane as it used to house the Corporation pack of hounds.[13]

Towards the end of the 18th century, merchants began to move away from the central area as it became more crowded with court property. A popular location was the slopes leading towards Everton, which offered spectacular views across the Mersey. One of those who moved was William Harper, Mayor in 1804 who lived in Rupert Lane (now covered by a recreation ground). He is remembered by **Harper Street**, which runs between Erskine Street and Prescot Street. Connecting these two streets at their bottom end is **Moss Street**, which was cut by banker John Moss of Whiston when he bought the land at the beginning of the 19th century. Richard Andrew Mould was a wine merchant who lived in the Kirkdale area. Around 1830 **Mould Street** was laid out in his honour, while parallel to this, **Dalrymple Street** remembers a book keeper and friend of his called William Dalrymple.

A timber merchant named Edward Mason moved to Edge Hill and paid for the construction of St. Mary's Church. He built a mansion and laid out **Mason Street** to its south. When the Liverpool to Manchester railway opened, its locomotive terminus was at Edge Hill, with the carriages then being horse drawn to the main station at Crown Street. The first Chairman of the railway company was merchant Charles Lawrence, who had been Mayor in 1823 and after whom **Lawrence Road** in Wavertree is named.

Josias Booker was a West India merchant who had settled in Poplar Grove in Allerton by 1828. He ran plantations in British Guyana and remained a leading figure in Liverpool until his death in 1865. He built some cottages for his farm workers and these became known as Bookers Lane and subsequently its present title of **Booker Avenue**. Thomas Littledale, Mayor in 1826 was buried in Knotty Ash churchyard in 1861. He lived in Highfield House in Broadgreen and **Littledale**, at the side of the church is named after him.

---

[13] Dogs kept by the Corporation for hunting.

## LOCAL GOVERNMENT FIGURES
## FROM 1835 ONWARDS

In 1835 there was a considerable shake up in Local Government when the Municipal Reform Act standardised council structures across the country. It also stipulated that councillors had to be elected by local ratepayers, as prior to this each authority was able to make its own arrangements. Whereas most Mayors from before this Act are remembered in the city centre, those after it tend to be commemorated further afield as Liverpool expanded with time. As well as Mayors and councillors, a number of high ranking council employees have also been honoured in Liverpool's street names.

One street in the city centre that is named after someone with local government connections is **Eberle Street**. Philip Eberle, who owned two hotels in Dale Street, acted as caterer to the Town Hall for 16 years in the second half of the 19th century after coming to Liverpool from Germany.

Only two members of the old Town Council were re-elected in the first Municipal Elections.[14] One of them was John Shaw Leigh, an attorney who inherited lands from his father. He lived at Edge Lane Hall from 1829 to 1835 and gave his name to **Leigh Street**, which now serves Wavertree Technology Park.

One of Liverpool's first Mayors after the 1835 Act was Hugh Hornby, in 1838. He was head of H & J Hornby & Co, which engaged in trade with Russia. Following his stint as Mayor, he went on to become Chairman of the Health Committee. Kent Street North, off Limekiln Lane in Vauxhall, was re-named **Hornby Street** in his honour. This street used to run right through to Vauxhall Road, but has now been considerably shortened by the building of Limekiln Lane Health Centre and Mother Teresa School. On the other side of the school, off Titchfield Street, a small section of the old line of the street remains and is now named **Hornby Walk**

Following on from Hugh Hornby as Mayor in 1839 was corn merchant Sir Joshua Walmsley. His family owned land in the Vauxhall area and **Walmsley Street** was named after him. At this time, Liverpool's docks were expanding northwards and a key figure behind this was James

---

[14] There were 48 members of the new council.

Holme, who suggested that land was purchased from the Earl of Derby. Despite being a councillor he devoted far more energy to dock activities and off Derby Road, near to Sandon Dock, **Holme Street** remembers him.

Off Shaw Street, **Langsdale Street** was named after Alderman Edward Langsdale. He represented the Everton ward and was Chairman of the Health Committee for many years in the mid 19th century, as well as being a member of the Dock Committee. Near to Liverpool FC's Anfield stadium is **Houlding Street**, named after the man who founded the club, John Houlding. Houlding was also a councillor and owned the Sandon Hotel, which is situated on the corner of the street. John Farnworth was a timber merchant and representative for South Toxteth who was Mayor in 1865, giving his name to **Farnworth Street**.

Richard C. Gardner, who was Mayor in 1862, had lived at Newsham House for some time after Liverpool Corporation purchased it in 1846. When Newsham Park was developed in the 1860s one of its main roads, **Gardners Drive**, was named after him. The much smaller **Gardner Road**, at the bottom end of West Derby Road, also remembers him. His sister Margaret married William Preston, a local councillor who had served as Mayor in 1858. They lived on the other side of Rocky Lane to Newsham Park in Rock House, which gave its name to **Rock House Street**. Just a few streets further up Rocky Lane are **Preston Grove** and **Ellel Grove**. The latter is named after Ellel Grange, an Italianate villa built by Preston in 1859 on land he purchased south of Lancaster. This house is now a listed building and the home of Ellel Ministries, a Christian Missionary Organisation. Nearby there is a **Grange Street**, as well as **Morecambe Street**, which is named after the nearest seaside town to Ellel Grange.

**Sheil Road** is named after Richard Sheil, the first Irish Alderman on Liverpool Council. **Holt Road** takes its name from George Holt, a councillor for West Derby who was a successful property developer. He was responsible for the first India Buildings in 1834 and co-founded the Lamport and Holt shipping line and also the Bank of Liverpool. Holt Road was developed on land owned by his father-in-law William Durning, after whom **Durning Road** is named. These three roads formed part of Liverpool's first ring road, which was developed in the

1860s to link the southern suburbs of Edge Hill and Toxteth with the northern ones of Anfield and Everton.

In Wavertree part of the old Wavertree Lane was re-named **Picton Road** in honour of councillor, architect and historian Sir James Allanson Picton. He lived in Wavertree and was Chairman of the Libraries and Museums Committee for nearly forty years, being knighted in 1881 for his public services. Two small streets off Picton Road are **Picton Crescent** and **Picton Grove**.

In the 19th century, a number of local libraries were developed in Liverpool, five of which were funded by philanthropist and steel magnate Andrew Carnegie (1835-1919). One of those was Lister Drive and the adjacent **Carnegie Road** was named in his honour. Born in Scotland, he emigrated from there to America when he was just 13 and went on to give over $350 million to educational and cultural projects worldwide.

John Woodruff was a councillor who owned a flourishing pawn broking business, as well as being a senior churchwarden of St Paul's church in Princes Park. Nearby, **Woodruff Street**, off Harlow Street is named after him. Another key pillar of St. Paul's church in the mid 19th century was James Robertson, who traded in timber and represented South Toxteth. **Robertson Street** remembers him, while Charles Henry Beloe, who represented Abercromby Ward from 1892 to 1902, was commemorated when Bright Street was changed to **Beloe Street** in his honour.

Ship builder Thomas Bland Royden was Mayor of Liverpool in 1879. While he was Mayor he entertained the Crown Prince of Sweden, who unveiled the Steble Fountain at the top of William Brown Street, which was erected following a donation by Lieutenant-Colonel Steble, Mayor in 1875. **Royden Street** and **Steble Street**, which are close to each other in Toxteth, commemorate both Mayors.

Francis Shand was Mayor in 1856. His father, William Shand had built Springwood House and owned forty acres of land in Allerton. Their merchanting concern traded in Barbados and **Shand Street** in Garston is named in the family's honour.

In 1907 William Benjamin Browning presented Liverpool Corporation with the Roby Hall Estate. From this Bowring Park was created and is now a golf course, with **Bowring Park Road** in Childwall being named after it. Bowring was the first elected Lord Mayor of Liverpool in 1894, having joined the council in 1884 following in his fathers footsteps. He was also head of C.T.Bowring & Co. ship owners, a company that is still in existence today under the umbrella of a much larger corporation.

During the first half of the 20th century, as Liverpool expanded further outward, rural areas such as Walton became swamped with new housing. A number of the main arterial routes built to serve these new estates were named after local civic dignitaries of the time. **Utting Avenue** and **Utting Avenue East** take their names from Sir John Utting, who was Mayor in 1917. He had served on the council from 1899 and was Chairman of the Hospitals Committee, taking a personal interest in the building of the Fazakerley Annexe fever hospital. A doctor, he wrote many papers concerning sanitary science and was also Chairman of the Port Sanitary Authority. **Muirhead Avenue** and **Muirhead Avenue East** are named after William Muirhead, Chairman of the Health Committee in the early 20th century. Prior to its development, Muirhead Avenue had once formed a tree lined entrance to Lark Hill Mansion, which stood on its corner with Queens Drive.

As Walton was developed, a famous local figure was remembered in **Richard Kelly Drive**. Kelly was born in Walton in 1839 and served as the local churchwarden, overseer and as a member of the local Conservative Association. He sat on the Walton Urban District Council and when Walton was absorbed into Liverpool he then represented Warbreck on the city council. In addition to all these duties he was also appointed a J.P. in 1893.

In the south of the city, two major routes are also named after former councillors. Alderman Thomas Menlove (1840-1913) was a Chairman of the Health Committee and gives his name to **Menlove Avenue**, which was once no more than a minor track to Woolton. Liverpool's Mayor in 1915, solicitor Arthur Stanley Mather is remembered by **Mather Avenue**. In the mid 19th century councillor and ironmonger Joseph Cooper lived in Oak house on Aigburth Hall Avenue. His memory lives on in **Cooper Avenue North** and **Cooper Avenue South**, while in the same vicinity **Brodie Avenue** is named after John Alexander Brodie, who was the City Engineer from 1898 to 1925. He developed Queens Drive, but also worked further afield and was responsible for the road system in New Delhi. A keen sports fan, he also patented football goal nets in 1890. An Irish councillor named Gregory Taggart gave his name to **Taggart Avenue** in Childwall after the district was absorbed into Liverpool in 1913. Originally this was called Park Road, after Stand Park, but the name was changed to avoid confusion with Park Road in Liverpool 8.

The naming of streets after councillors has still taken place in more recent times. In the late 1980s **Paul Orr Court** was built in the Eldonian Village. This was named after Paul Orr, a long standing councillor for the Vauxhall area. He continued to serve the local community and even after resigning from the Labour Party he still stood as an independent candidate in May 2000, despite being over 80 years old. However, he was beaten into second place in the poll. Paul Orr donated the upturned beer crates that were used as chairs in Liverpool FC's famous 'bootroom', having given trainer Joe Fagan some stout as a thank you for allowing his amateur team to receive treatment at Anfield. Rosemary Cooper, after whom **Rosemary Close** off Grove Street is named, was Lord Mayor 1992-3 and while in office a large scale re-development programme in the area, Project Rosemary, was put into operation. Rosemary served as a councillor for nearly 25 years and is a member of the board of directors of the nearby Liverpool Women's Hospital.

# MARITIME INFLUENCES

Liverpool's dock system was developed in the 18th century, with canals then being built to transport goods from inland for export. In addition, shipbuilding flourished as merchants required more and more vessels. With the onset of steam in the 19th century, great shipping lines were formed in the city, transporting freight and passengers to all corners of the world. Sadly, the canals have fallen into disuse, the nearest shipyards are now in Birkenhead and air travel has now vastly reduced the numbers of ships seen on the Mersey. However, street names have left us with many reminders of Liverpool's shipbuilding past around the city, as well as of canals and the great liners that sailed from the port around the turn of the 19th century.

Liverpool's first Dock Engineer was Thomas Steers, who built the first dock in 1715. This involved the draining of the Pool, leading to the formation of **Paradise Street** on land owned by Steers. He named it after a street in Rotherhithe, London where he once lived. A shipwright, Thomas Hurst, who provided timber for construction of the dock is remembered by **Hurst Street** while a descendant of Steers, Spencer, is commemorated by **Spencer Street** and **Steers Street** in Everton. Steers successor was Henry Berry, who lived at the top of Duke Street and is remembered by **Berry Street**. He masterminded the Sankey Canal, which linked Liverpool with St. Helens and gave its name to **Sankey Street**. Perhaps the most famous Dock Engineer was Jesse Hartley in the mid 19th century. His most well known work is the Albert Dock and one of its roadways, **Hartley Quay**, remembers its builder.

Francis Egerton, 3rd Duke of Bridgewater, developed Dukes Dock in 1773 to export his textiles. The road leading to this, **Gower Street**, is named after his brother in law, while **Bridgewater Street** was named after the completion of the Bridgewater Canal that linked Liverpool to Manchester in 1776. This was an extension of an earlier canal, which had been built to carry coal from Bridgewater's mines in Worsley to his factories in Manchester. **Brindley Street** remembers James Brindley, the surveyor of both the Bridgewater Canal and the Trent and Mersey Canal.

The Leeds and Liverpool Canal connected Liverpool with Leeds and the mill towns of Lancashire and Yorkshire. Although it now terminates near Burlington Street, it originally ran to nearly as far as Old Hall Street and gave its name to **Leeds Street**, which was developed in the late 19th century on the site of a former road called Maidens Green. Nearby, there had been another Leeds Street named after the canal, which then became **Old Leeds Street**. Nearly 100 years later in the 1980s new developments in the Vauxhall area were **Canalside Grove** and **Lockfields View**.

**Grayson Street** is named after a shipwright called Edward Grayson, whose works, H & C Grayson were on the site of the Albert Dock. Grayson, who was Mayor in 1770, was killed in a duel in 1804, the last but one to be fought in Liverpool. His killer was William Sparling, whose family are remembered in nearby **Sparling Street**, which was in existence by 1785 and named after a Mr Sparling's shipyard. Also in this area is **Carpenters Row**, which commemorates the carpenters who worked in the local shipyards. One of the many uses for ships built in 18th Century Liverpool was the whaling industry. Baffin Street, which is no longer in existence, ran alongside Queens Dock, where ships would have come back to with their catch. This was named after Baffin Bay, off the Greenland coast. However, there is still a **Greenland Street**, running off St. James Street in the direction of Queens Dock. These streets were so named as the whaling trade started to look further away for its catch after supplies near Norway became exhausted.

In the 2nd quarter of the 19th century William Laird developed Birkenhead almost single handed. After first living in Liverpool when he came down to England from Scotland, he realised the potential of the Wirral side of the Mersey and moved there in 1824, opening his first shipyard at Wallasey Pool in 1828. Liverpool did not forget him however and **Laird's Place**, off Burlington Street in Vauxhall is named after him. On the Springwood Estate in Allerton there is a **Brocklebank Lane**. This takes its name from Thomas Brocklebank who lived in Springwood House from 1844 to 1906. He had acquired his wealth through his grandfather, who had built shipyards in Whitehaven in the 18th century. Another member of the family was Ralph Brocklebank, who was Chairman of the Mersey Docks and Harbour Board from 1863 to 1869 and was succeeded on his retirement by Thomas Langton, a partner in T & W Earle, American merchants. He was also Chairman of the Pacific Steamship Company and **Langton Street** in Wavertree is named after him.

As the 19th century wore on, shipping lines rather than shipbuilders became more prominent in Liverpool, as the passenger trade grew. One example of a yard to close was Thomas Royden & Sons, which had been started in 1818 by Thomas Royden after he came to Liverpool as a 16 years old shipyard apprentice in 1808. His company was situated on the site of the Queens Dock Customs and Excise Building and developed into a nationwide leader in the construction of large iron sailing ships. In the late 19th century his son, Thomas Bland Royden closed it down and then founded the Indra Line of steamships, which traded between London and New Zealand, the Far East and USA. The Royden family are remembered by **Royden Way**, which leads into the Brunswick Business Park, while other shipping lines to be commemorated here are **Harrison Way** and **Ellerman Road**, named after the Harrison and Ellerman Lines respectively.

In 1840, the first Cunard service out of Liverpool left bound for Halifax and Boston and the company later had their headquarters in the Cunard Building on the waterfront. Cunard's influence in Liverpool can be seen in Walton, where a small group of streets are named after their ships. **Ivernia Road** and **Saxonia Road** are named after sister ships which sailed between Liverpool and Boston, while **Sylvania Road** takes its name from a ship that carried cargo on the same route. **Lusitania Road** and **Mauretania Road** are named after two 'superliners' that took passengers from Liverpool to New York. The Mauretania held the westbound and eastbound speed crossing records for twenty years until 1929 while the Lusitania, which was the largest vessel in the world when launched in 1906, was torpedoed off the coast of Ireland in 1915. This act by a German u-boat cost 1,200 lives and led to Cunard suspending Atlantic passenger services during the First World War.

In Garston, more Cunard ships that sailed between Liverpool and America have been remembered. **Campania Street** and **Lucania Street** are named after sister ships that were the largest in the world when built in 1893. The Lucania was destroyed by fire in Huskisson Dock in 1909 while the Campania sank after a collision with a battleship in 1918 following its sale to the navy for use as a troop ship. Two other sister ships are remembered by **Etruria Street** and **Umbria Street**. They were the last Cunard ships to have sails and remained in service until being scrapped in 1910. **Carpathia Street** is named after a ship most famous for rescuing survivors from the Titanic, while **Caronia Street** takes its name from one of the first ships in the world to be fitted with watertight doors. All the ships mentioned so far carried passengers from Liverpool to New York, but one liner that sailed from Liverpool to Boston gives its name to **Ultonia Street**. This ship was a cargo steamer on the route but after moving to the Trieste-New York route in 1904, it eventually sank after being hit by a German torpedo in 1917, all bar one of the people on board being saved.

Another shipping line based in Liverpool was the City of Dublin Steam Packet Company, which ran passenger and mail services between Liverpool and Ireland. Their berth was near to **Dublin Street**, while in Old Swan four of the company's ships are remembered by **Belfast Road, Leinster Road, Munster Road** and **Ulster Road**.

# LIVERPOOL'S BIG HOUSES

As Liverpool became more crowded during the late 18th Century, many merchants began to move away from the town to countryside areas such as Everton or Wavertree. These houses were usually built near to main roads so they could still get to Liverpool quite easily when necessary. With the onset of railways in the 19th century, wealthy traders were able to move even further away from the inner city area and commute to their business premises. Many of these large houses are still in existence today, or alternatively leave their legacy behind in the naming of streets.

West India merchant George Campbell built an ecclesiastic looking mansion in Everton and named it St Domingo House after a French ship he had captured off the coast of San Domingo. The house was demolished after Campbell's death in 1773, but John Sparling built another in its place and lived there until his death in 1800. The property was then leased out by his son and eventually became a school. Situated on its corner with Beacon Lane, it gave its name to St. Domingo Lane, which was then an unnamed continuation north of Heyworth Street and is now known as **St Domingo Road**. The estates grounds stretched as far as Walton Breck Road and **St Domingo Vale** and **St Domingo Grove** also take their names from the house. A wine merchant, Samuel Woodhouse owned a house called Bronte near to Everton Valley, which gave its name to **Bronte Street** off London Road.

In Tuebrook, the Larkhill mansion was built for merchant and colliery owner Jonathan Blundell. It was purchased by banker Richard Heywood in 1776 and remained in his family's hands for over one hundred years, before becoming a branch library for Liverpool City Council. It was demolished in 1962 but has given its name to **Larkhill Lane.** One of the lanes within the estate was **Lisburn Lane**, which is still in existence today, being given that name as it led to Lisburn Farm. A house called Barnfield used to exist on the site of the Jolly Miller pub on Queens Drive. This is remembered today by **Barnfield Drive**, which came into existence shortly after the 2nd World War. The Jolly Miller's name originates from the ancient mill that stood at the top of **Millbank**. This mill gave its name to a house and subsequently the road of the same name.

In 1855 Russian consul Philip Blessig built Blackmoor Hall on the site of Blackmoor Moss in West Derby. This was demolished in the 1920s, giving rise to **Blackmoor Drive**. A Georgian house in West Derby came into the hands of Lawrence Heyworth, a merchant, in the early 19th century. He built a tree house in a yew tree in its garden and the house then became known as Yew Tree House. This then gave the name to the road it stood on, **Yew Tree Lane**. Another merchants house in West Derby was Bellefield, once owned by East India merchant Sir Edward Bates. **Bellefield Drive** was named after this, but it was closed off from Sandfield Park as Bates refused to pay for the upkeep of roads there in return for access to it. It remains like this today.

Scarisbrick House stood in Norris Green and was owned by the Scarisbrick family of Scarisbrick Hall, near Ormskirk. **Scarisbrick Crescent, Scarisbrick Drive, Scarisbrick Road** and **Scarisbrick Place** all take their names from this house. The road on which it was situated, **Strawberry Road**, took its name from Strawberry Farm in the early 19th Century, although it was then known as Strawberry Lane. In Fazakerley, **Sparrow Hall Road** does not take its named from a grand property. Sparrow Hall was a black and white cottage that stood on the corner of Long Lane and Lower Lane, but nicknamed such due to the birds that used to nest in its thatched roof.

**Spellow Lane** in Walton takes its name from Spellow House, which was owned by the Fazakerley family of Fazakerley Hall in Lower Lane. Spellow House was built in the 13th century, not demolished until 1860 and its name has origins from Viking times. **Fazakerley Road** was the orginal driveway to Fazakerley House, a three storey stone farmhouse built in 1749. **Evered Avenue** remembers Miss Evered, who owned the house at the start of the 20th century and was a relative of the Fazakerley family. The house, along with its grounds, was subsequently sold to Liverpool Corporation and demolished. The Rice family, who were related by marriage to the Fazakerleys, had a house called Rice House, which stood close to the Breeze Hill flyover. **Rice Lane** remembers the family and house.

The original name for **Hall Lane** in Edge Hill was Mount Vernon, named due to its slope and its proximity to Vernon's Hall, an 18th century or earlier structure. The name was changed in the mid 19th century but the name of the long gone hall has survived in a number of smaller streets in the area bearing the name, the most significant of which is **Mount Vernon**.

A doctor named Samuel Solomon, who practiced in Marybone developed a herbal medicine named the 'balm of gilead', which he produced from a secret recipe. He built a mansion named Gilead House, off Kensington, from the proceeds of this. When this was demolished **Balm Street, Gilead Street** and **Solomon Street** were named in his honour.

In Broadgreen, merchant Joseph Leigh built Oak Hill House in 1773, standing between what is now Rossall Road and Saville Road. It was named after some oak trees were brought here from the ladies walk[15] in Old Hall Street in 1778. The last tenant of the house was timber merchant Edward Chaloner. The house was demolished in the early 20th century and its name lives on in **Oakhill Park, Oakhill Road** and **West Oakhill Park**. The Newsham Molineux family, who are commemorated by **Molineux Avenue**, owned the Staplands mansion, after which **Staplands Road** is named. However, their main residence was at Newsham Park and **Molyneux Road**, off Sheil Road remembers them there. This family is no relation to the Molyneux family who were the earls of Sefton and lived at Croxteth Hall.

The district of Dovecot takes its name from Dovecote House, built in 1829 by John Tarbock on the junction of Pilch Lane and **Dovecot Avenue**, which also has a **Dovecot Place** off it. It was later occupied by a cotton merchant named Adam Dugdale and had been named after an earlier house of the same name which was demolished in the 18th century. The name dovecote comes from a building, which would have been used by the lord of the manor for housing doves, which were a source of winter food. Richard Gildart built Finch House in 1776 after buying land from the earl of Sefton. Mockbeggar Lane, on which it stood, then became **Finch Lane**. The house was eventually demolished in 1912 after coming into the hands of the earls of Derby and **Finch Dene, Finch Way** and **Finch Close** also take their names from it.

James Clements, who was Mayor in 1775 built Ashfield House off the 'road to Wavertree' (later Picton Road). **Ashfield** takes its name from

---

[15] A tree lined walk with views which was exclusive to ladies.

this, as well as **Ash Grove, Ash Close** and **Ash Vale**. Wavertree playground was created in 1895 following the anonymous donation of a derelict house and its grounds called 'The Grange' to the City of Liverpool. This is why the playing fields are often referred to as 'The Mystery'. The house, in which Prince Alfred, son of Queen Victoria, stayed in 1866 was demolished in 1895 but **Grange Terrace** means its name still lives on. **Lance Lane** took its name from Lance Cottage, which was named by insurance broker Thomas Lance (1769-1829). **Heathfield Road** was named after Heathfield, a house owned in the early 20th century by solicitor William Watson Rutherford (see also 'Liverpool's MPs and Prime Ministers').

A public inquiry in 1998 was held into the future of Sandown Hall in Olive Lane, Wavertree, as its new owners wanted to demolish it for new housing. Two years later, Deputy Prime Minister John Prescott reluctantly gave the go ahead for this as the hall had fallen into disrepair and it was demolished in November 2000. Built in the early 1800s, it came into the hands of Crawford Biscuits in the 1920s for use as its sports and social club. The hall gave its name to Sandown Park, a private 19th century residential estate containing a number of mansions. **Sandown Road** takes its name from the estate while **Crawford Drive** is in relation to its one time owner. **Sandown Lane**, which leads to the Sandown Park estate, was first proposed in 1803 but it was some years before it got developed. Its varying stages of development mean that many different architectural styles are featured in the road.

A mansion called Westdale House used to stand at the junction of Rathbone Road and Sunningdale Road. Its last owner was cotton broker John Stock and after 1910, new roads were laid out including **Westdale Road**. The dale theme continues as **Eastdale Road, Northdale Road** and **Southdale Road** all took their names from this one house, as do **Mindale Road, Standale Road** and **Sunningdale Road**.

One of Liverpool's oldest structures is the Monkswell, at the corner of North Drive and Mill Lane in Wavertree. It is reputed to be over 600 years old and gave its name to Monkswell House that stood nearby, from which **Monkswell Drive** is named. Another house near here was Valencia House, which made way for **Valencia Road** in the 1930s. This house was once the home of a fruit broker named William M. George, who may have named it after the Spanish city of Valencia that is an important centre for agricultural trading.

In 1790 Olive Mount House was built. Now used as health authority offices, it is not certain what was named first, Olive Mount hill or house. The house has given its name to **Olive Mount Road** and **Olive Mount Walk**, while its surrounding buildings, which formed a children's hospital, were demolished in the 1990s to make way for **Crossley Drive, Hollins Close** and **Swan Crescent**. These three new streets were named at the suggestion of the local Wavertree Society after Luke Crossley, who lived there in 1841, Francis Hollins, a cotton broker who lived there in 1871 and James Swan, a tea dealer who built the house.

Eton Lodge in Childwall has been a home for Catholic bishops since 1851, but its intended purpose when it was built 75 years earlier was as a school, the 'Eton of the North'. **Cromptons Lane** is named after Dr. Peter Crompton, one of its former owners. Dudlow Hall gave is name to **Dudlow Lane, Dudlow Drive** and **Dudlow Gardens**, while **Dudlow Nook Road** now marks the edge of what was the Dudlow Estate. At the top of Taggart Avenue was Stand House, which is now the site of shops. The land surrounding the house was known as Stand Park and is now a Liverpool Hope University College campus, but its name lives on in **Stand Park Road**. Another large house, Hill Top stood at the top of Childwall Priory Road. This was once the home of Colonel Henry Concanon, Assistant General Manager of the White Star Line. When the house was demolished before the 2nd World War, **Hilltop Road** was named in its memory.

The district of Belle Vale takes its name from Belle Vale Hall, which stood at the corner of Wambo Lane and **Belle Vale Road**. Lee Hall, which stood on the site of Lee Park golf course, was built for ship builder John Okill in 1773 and demolished in 1956. One of its residents during the 19th century was John Hayes Wilson, a Chairman of the Liverpool Water Committee who was involved in the construction of Liverpool's main water supply at Lake Vrynwy The hall gives its name to the surrounding district as well as **Lee Hall Road**. On the other side of the golf course in Netherley, **Garden Lodge Grove** takes its name from Garden Lodge, which was built in 1841. **Holt Lane**, which is named after Holt Hall farm, runs to an adult training centre and then becomes a pedestrian track leading to the clubhouse of Childwall golf course.

The Grange mansion in Rose Brow, Gateacre was re-built in 1865 on the site of an earlier house by Sir Andrew Barclay Walker. He was Mayor of Liverpool in 1873, 1876 and 1877, as well as being the owner of Walkers Warrington brewery. He also gave money for the building of the Walker Art Gallery in William Brown Street in the city centre. At the time of writing, the house stands empty although the new owner plans to convert it into apartments. Its previous uses include being used as a seamen's home and nursing home and it gives its name to one of the main roads in Gateacre, **Grange Lane**, as well as **Grangeside** and **Grange Way**. Gateacre Hall is now a hotel and is situated at the bottom of **The Nook**, which was the original name for the hall. The former name for the Grange Manor (now a function suite) was Gorsey Cop, which is still remembered by **Gorsey Cop Road** and **Gorsey Cop Way**. Other houses, which are now long demolished, that have given their names to streets in Gateacre are Elmsfield, (**Elmsfield Close**) and Orient House, (**Orient Drive**).

In Woolton, a local solicitor by the name of Ambrose Lee laid out **Beaconsfield Road** in the 1860s to lead to his mansion, Beaconsfield. Off Menlove Avenue, **The Vineries** is named after an estate that was once the residence of a Thomas Charles Clarke and was unfit for occupation by the early 20th century. Many of the houses in the Woolton and Gateacre area were built using stone from Woolton Quarry, which was opened by James Rose, a self made man who was born in 1783 and married well. The quarry is still remembered by **Quarry Street, The Old Quarry** and **Rockmount Close**, while Rose himself built **Rose Street**.

In 1847 merchant Joseph Hornby purchased some land east of Menlove Avenue. A house was then designed by Lonsdale Elmes and named Druids Cross House, presumably due to the proximity of the Calder Stones, which may be 3-4,000 years old. **Druids Cross Road** was formally adopted in 1868 and the house has also given its name to **Druids Cross Gardens, Druids Park** and **Druidsville Road,** while **Hornby Lane** commemorated Joseph Hornby himself.

The Harthill Estate, which is now Liverpool's botanic gardens, is in Calderstones Park. In the grounds of this stood Harthill House, which was built in 1825 and has given its name to **Harthill Avenue** and

**Harthill Road**. This was bought in 1848 by iron and copper merchant John Bibby, son-in-law of dock engineer Jesse Hartley. After his death in 1899 it later became a police headquarters before its demolition in 1937 after dry rot was found.

The **Allerton Beeches** mansion, which gives its name to a road of the same name, was demolished in 1939, having been built for sugar refiner Sir Henry Tate (1819-99). This mansion was built on the site of another large house called Greenhill, after which **Greenhill Road** is named. Further down Allerton Road, opposite Yew Tree Road, stood **Verdala Towers**, another house that is copied by a road name. Its first tenant, Charles McIver Junior in 1870, gave the house its unusual name, naming it after a tower in Malta that literally means 'tower of the greenfields.' **Yew Tree Road** was laid out as a private road by Ambrose Lace in 1864 and named after Yew Tree Farm. Off this road is **Dowsefield Lane**, which led to Dowsefield, a house built by a Hermann J. Sillemm and named after Dowse House farm.

The origins of **Carnatic Road** in Mossley Hill go back to 1778 when a French ship, the Carnatic, was captured by a privateer[16] called the Mentor, captained by John Dawson. The prize included raw silk, coffee and tea and from the proceeds of this Peter Baker, owner of the Mentor, was able to build Carnatic Hall. This hall burnt down in 1889 and a new one built on its site, which was pulled down in 1964 to make way for the University of Liverpool student residences that bear the same name. Within the grounds of Carnatic Hall stood Elmswood Hall, which now gives its name to **Elmswood Road**. This road was in existence in the 18th century as an unnamed lane that connected to Rose Lane.

Also in Mossley Hill, **Briarwood Road** takes its name from a house of the same name that stood on Carnatic Road. At the turn of the 20th century Joseph Ainsworth Woods, a dental surgeon, lived there. Nearby, **Kelton Grove** is named after a house still in existence, which is now a Nugent Care training centre. **North Sudley Road** was re-named along with **South Sudley Road** after the creation of a sports ground on Barkhill Road split the original Sudley Road in two. This was named after Sudley Hall, which is now an art gallery. The hall was purchased by shipping magnate George Holt (see Holt Road) in 1883 and was left

---

[16] Ship that would operate under goverment licence and hunt down merchant vessels of hostile nations.

to the City of Liverpool by his daughter Emma Holt in 1944 after she died leaving no siblings. **Pitville Road** and **Pitville Avenue** take their names from a house called Pitville, which stood on the site of the University Sports Ground that the roads now surround.

Two buildings now owned by Liverpool John Moores University gave their names to **Barkhill Road** and **Holmefield Road**. Irene M. Marsh purchased the mansion of Barkhill in the early 20th century for her training college for women physical education teachers. It later became known as the I.M. Marsh College and expanded in 1947 when Holmefield House, a grade II listed building once occupied by shipping magnate and MP Sir Thomas Bland Royden, was purchased. The college became part of the then Liverpool Polytechnic in 1983 and although this became Liverpool John Moores University in 1992, the I.M. Marsh College has retained a separate identity within it.

**The Elms** in Toxteth was named after a house of the same name. The house was built around 1840 and had six elm trees in its grounds. Another mansion in this area was Fairview, which has given its name to **Fairview Place**.

Aigburth Hall was a medieval building that came into the hands of the Tarleton family through marriage. This was demolished around 1840 and a new hall was built which has also since been demolished. The hall, which was once the home of City Engineer J A Brodie gives its name to **Aigburth Hall Avenue** and **Aigburth Hall Road**. Off Aigburth Hall Avenue is **Oakland Road**, its name taken from the Oaklands mansion, home of merchant Richard Harrison from 1810 to 1840. It was also a home of Sir Alfred Lewis Jones, founder of the Liverpool School of Tropical Medicine. The hunting lodge of the mansion still stands on the bend of Holmefield Road, opposite the Grange hotel.

In 1844 shipbuilder Thomas Brocklebank bought Springwood House from William Shand and lived there until he died in 1906, aged 92. The 121-acre estate was bought by Liverpool Corporation in 1921 for development, but the house itself remains and is now a nursing home. **Springwood Avenue** takes its name from the house. At the turn of the twentieth century, a house called Melbreck stood at the junction of

**Melbreck Road** and Greenhill Road. **Cleveley Road** and **Cleveley Park** takes their names from Cleveley, built by cotton merchant Joseph Leather but demolished in 1965.

# LIVERPOOL'S MPS AND PRIME MINISTERS

People either from or associated with Liverpool have made great contributions to national politics. Whether they were born in Liverpool, represented the city or just owned land locally, they have all had their mark left permanently in local street names.

The earliest Liverpool street to be named after an MP was **Sir Thomas Street**, laid out as Sir Thomas Buildings in the late 17th century on land belonging to Sir Thomas Johnson. Johnson had been Mayor in 1695 and went on to be MP for the town from 1701 to 1723. While at Parliament, he brought in the Bill for the construction of Liverpool's first dock. The Municipal Buildings are on the site of his house and his memory is preserved in a tablet there. John Hardman was MP for Liverpool when he died in 1755. He had bought Allerton Hall (now a pub/restaurant) and owned land through which **Hardman Street** was later laid. This street was named after his widow Jane, who died in 1795 at the age of 92 She had given a large portion of her life to charity after all four of her children died before reaching adulthood.

**Gascoyne Street** in Vauxhall is named after Isaac Gascoyne, who represented Liverpool in Parliament from 1796 to 1831. Despite campaigns throughout the country for abolition, he continued to defend the slave trade, as he felt it was essential to Liverpool's economy. His brother, Bamber Gascoyne Junior had been MP from 1780 to 1796 and was preceded by Richard Pennant, who served in the Commons from 1767 to 1780. Pennant was also against abolition of the slave trade and was created Lord Penrhyn in 1783, giving his name to **Penrhyn Street** in Everton.

The only central Liverpool MP to become Prime Minister was George Canning, who in 1827 held the post for four months until his death. He had earlier been Foreign Secretary and Leader of the House of Commons. In the 1830's **Canning Street** was developed in his honour, while down near the waterfront **Canning Place** remembers him.

One of the most famous MPs to be remembered in Liverpool is William Huskisson, after whom **Huskisson Street** was named in the 1830's. He was a local MP from 1822 to 1830 and President of the Board of Trade, a role that enabled him to represent the interests of Liverpool's merchants by reducing duties on cotton and sugar. Unfortunately he has gone down in history more for being the first person to be killed in a railway passenger accident. During the opening of the Liverpool & Manchester Railway in 1830, the train stopped for a break at Parkside, near Newton-le-Willows. He crossed the line to speak to the Duke of Wellington but was struck by the locomotive. His injuries were so severe he died later that day. He is buried in a circular tomb, which still stands in the gardens to the rear of the Anglican Cathedral.

**Creswell Street**, off Everton Road, is named after Cresswell Cresswell who was one of Liverpool's two MPs from 1837 to 1842. Sir Howard Douglas represented the town for the next five years having earlier enjoyed a distinguished naval career. **Sir Howard Street, Sir Howard Way** and **Back Sir Howard Street** in Liverpool 8 remember him.

Dudley Ryder, Viscount Sandon, had been elected MP for Liverpool at the same time as Cresswell Cresswell. Linking Faulkner Street and Upper Parliament Street is **Sandon Street**, while one of the docks developed on the North Shore was also named Sandon Dock to commemorate him. Near to this is **Sandon Way**, which is off Derby Road on the Sandon Industrial Estate. In 1847 Viscount Sandon succeeded to the earldom of Harrowby and had to give up his seat in the Commons, but he remained in politics and was later made Chancellor of the Duchy of Lancaster. His son, also Viscount Sandon went on to become an MP in Liverpool, from 1868 until his father's death in 1882. He then succeeded to the earldom and **Harrowby Street** in Toxteth is named after him. This initially continued right through to Kingsley Road but has been reduced over time. What remains at the top end is now called **Harrowby Close.**

Despite being born in Ireland and representing South Lancashire in Parliament, William Brown did make his mark in Liverpool. He had come to Liverpool to establish a branch of his father's merchants firm and paid for the building of the William Brown Library, laying the foundation stone in 1857. When the building opened in 1860, the street in which it was situated, Shaws Brow, was re-named **William Brown Street**. The streets previous name had come from Samuel Shaw, who had established an 18th century pottery in the street. The family of Thomas Brassey (1836-1918) who served as MP for Hastings from 1868 to 1884 and unsuccessfully fought for the Abercomby seat a year later is remembered by **Brassey Street** in Toxteth. His father, also Thomas was a railway contractor who was born in Chester and lived in Birkenhead. He built lines all over the world, including Africa and India and left £3.2 million in his will when he died in 1870.

Born in Liverpool, William Ewart Gladstone had four terms as Prime Minister between 1868 and 1894, more than any other. **Gladstone Street**, off Vauxhall Road is named after him, as is a street of the same name in Edge Hill. There is also a **Gladstone Road** in Walton and Garston.

Edward Whitley served as leader of the Conservatives on Liverpool council before his election in 1880 as MP for Everton. **Whitley Street** in Vauxhall remembers him. George Goschen, who had earlier served as Chancellor of the Exchequer, was elected MP for Liverpool Exchange in 1887. He is remembered in Anfield and Old Swan, which both have a **Goschen Street**. William Watson Rutherford was a solicitor who lived in Wavertree and was Lord Mayor of Liverpool in 1902. The following year he was elected MP for West Derby and **Rutherford Road**, off Queens Drive in Mossley Hill, is named after him.

The 3rd Marquis of Salisbury, Robert Gascoyne Cecil, owner of Childwall Hall was Prime Minister from 1886 to 1892 and 1895 to 1902. He is not commemorated in the immediate city centre area (Salisbury Street near Islington is named after his forefathers), but in Wavertree a number of streets are named after him, the most obvious ones being **Salisbury Road** and **Cecil Street**. **Cranbourne Road** takes its name from the title of Viscount Cranborne that was given to the Marquis of Salisbury's eldest son. Cecil had assumed this in 1865 on the death of his brother. **Alderson Road** is named in honour of his wife, Georgina Alderson, while **Childwall Avenue** commemorates Childwall Hall, which had been built in the 18th century by Bamber Gascoyne. The hall was sold to Liverpool Corporation in 1947 but demolished when extensive dry rot was found. Salisbury's son Edgar was given the title Viscount Cecil of Chelwood in 1923 after a 17 year Parliamentary career, during which he served as Assistant Secretary of State for Foreign Affairs. He went on to represent British interests in the League of Nations and is remembered in Childwall by **Chelwood Avenue**.

# NATIONAL POLITICIANS

A number of Liverpool's streets are named after Prime Ministers and prominent politicians. Generally speaking, the more recent politicians are commemorated further away from the city centre, showing how the city has expanded over the years.

The first Prime Minister to be commemorated by a street name in Liverpool city centre was William Pitt The Elder, 1st Earl of Chatham who was in office from 1766 to 1768. **Pitt Street** had been laid out in his honour in 1765, before he became Prime Minister, in recognition of his distinguished political career that had begun in 1735. A later continuation of Pitt Street was **Upper Pitt Street**. His son, William Pitt the Younger, was Prime Minister from 1783 to 1801 and 1804 to 1806. He died while in office and Great Pitt Street was named in his honour, although this was soon changed to **Pomona Street**. Around the same time, **Chatham Street** was developed and was perhaps named after his father's title, given the fact that no title had yet been bestowed upon him.

Outside the city centre, an earlier Prime Minister than Pitt the Elder to be remembered was John Stuart, Earl of Bute, who gave his name to **Bute Street** in Everton. He was in office for only eleven months from 1762 to 1763 before being forced to resign due to gossip about his private life. Augustus Henry Fitzroy, the 3rd Duke of Grafton, was another Prime Minister who was forced to resign due to attacks on his private life after three years in office from 1767 to 1770. He gave his name to **Fitzroy Way** in Everton, as well as **Grafton Street** in Toxteth.

Lord North, 2nd Earl of Guilford was Prime Minster from 1770 to 1782, resigning after Britain's defeat in the American War of Independence. **North Street**, off Dale Street is named after him, as is **Guilford Close** in Everton. This has replaced an earlier Guilford Street and is one of a number in the vicinity named after Prime Ministers of the pre Victorian era. Charles Wentworth succeeded Guilford, but died in office after only a few months allowing William Petty, Marquiss of Landsdowne, to take over. Landsdowne restored peace with America and is remembered by **Landsdowne Place**. Robert Banks Jenkinson, 2nd Earl of Liverpool, was Prime Minister from 1812 to 1827, winning four general elections before finally resigning after suffering a stroke. **Jenkinson Street** was named after him. In addition to the streets in Everton that are named after Prime Ministers, there is a **Downing Street** and **Premier Street**. The original Downing Street in London takes its name from Sir George Downing who was Secretary of the Treasury in 1667.

Staying in Everton, there are a number of streets that have been named after politicians and members of the public who were active in the campaign for Parliamentary reform in the 18th century, when very few people were allowed to vote. Charles Fox, who was Lord of the Treasury under Lord North, is remembered by **Fox Street**. He was against the slave trade and a promoter of Catholic Emancipation.[17] In 1794 he denounced the trial of lawyer John Horne Tooke, who was charged with High Treason after trying to organise a convention for supporters of reform. Tooke, who was found not guilty, is commemorated in **Horne Street** and there was once a Tooke Street in existence. **Richmond Row** is named after another reformist, Charles Lennox, Duke of Richmond, who tried to introduce a reform bill to Parliament in 1780 but found no support. He testified at the trial of Tooke and was forced to admit his previous radical views for reform and as a result had to resign from his position in the government. One man who fared worse was Scottish reformist William Skirving, after whom **Skirving Street** is named. He was transported to Australia in 1794 for distributing leaflets in Edinburgh urging reform and died soon after arriving.

William Wyndham Baron Grenville who introduced the bill to Parliament for the abolition of slavery, served as Prime Minister from 1806 to 1807. **Grenville Street South** in the city centre remembers him, but for a short time in the mid 19th century this was named Leveson Street. This is due to boundary changes in 1835 that saw Everton absorbed into Liverpool. As a Grenville Street existed in Everton, the street name in Liverpool was changed to avoid confusion. However, after the brutal murder of four people in the street in 1849, the name was changed back and the suffix south added due to the notoriety the street was attracting.

Grenville was succeeded as Prime Minister by William Henry Cavendish Bentinck, 3rd Duke of Portland, who has four streets in the Vauxhall area named after him. They are **Bentinck Street, Portland**

---

[17] Catholic Emancipation - granting of more civil rights to Catholics, including the right to vote.

**Street, Titchfield Street** and **Woodstock Street**. The latter two streets come from two of his other titles, Marquis of Titchfield and Viscount Woodstock. He was Prime Minister from 1807 to 1809 after serving as Home Secretary from 1794 to 1801.

Bentinck's Lord Chancellor was John Scott, 1st Earl of Eldon, who is also remembered in Vauxhall by **Eldon Street, Eldon Grove** and **Eldon Place**. He held the position between 1801 and 1827, except for a brief interlude in 1806-7 when Thomas Erskine, 1st Baron Erskine was in the post. Erskine, after whom **Erskine Street** in Everton is named, famously saved a madman who tried to shoot King George III from the death penalty on the grounds of insanity. This led to a change in the legal attitude towards criminal responsibility.

**Brougham Terrace** was the venue for many Liverpool marriages until the summer of 2000. This was named after Henry Peter Brougham, 1st Baron Brougham and Vaux (1778-1868). As a lawyer he defended Caroline of Brunswick against divorce proceedings brought against her by the Government (on behalf of George IV). He was elected to Parliament in 1810 and advocated liberal causes such as promotion of popular education. He was later Lord Chancellor from 1830 to 1834.

In Toxteth **Beaconsfield Street** commemorates Benjamin Disraeli, Earl of Beaconsfield who led the country from 1874 to 1880. Next to Beaconsfield Street is **Cairns Street**, named after Lord Cairns who was Disraeli's Lord Chancellor. In another area of Toxteth **Peel Street** is named after Sir Robert Peel, Prime Minister 1834-5 and 1841-6. He was founder of the modern Conservative Party as well as having been responsible for the introduction of a modern police force while he had been Home Secretary in 1829.

Further south, the centre of Garston can boast a cluster of streets named after Prime Ministers. In addition to **Gladstone Road, Palmerston Road** (Viscount Palmerston PM 1855-65) and **Russell Road** (Earl Russell, PM 1865-6) are both named after Victorian leaders, with **Clarendon Road** being named after Lord Clarendon, Foreign Secretary in the 1850's. **Wellington Street** is named in honour of the Duke of Wellington, who went on to serve as Prime Minister on two separate occasions after his victory over Napoleon at Waterloo in 1815.

Spencer Compton Cavendish, 8th Duke of Devonshire and Marquis of Hartington succeeded Gladstone as Liberal leader in 1875, only to hand the post back to him in 1880. **Cavendish Drive** in Walton and **Hartington Road** in Toxteth remember him. Spencer's father William Cavendish was also Earl of Burlington, giving his name to **Burlington Street** in Vauxhall. Going back even further, Spencer's grandfather, William George Cavendish was commemorated in Princes Park by **Devonshire Road** and **Devonshire Road West**. They were named as William's horticulturist Joseph Paxton designed the park. **Chatsworth Drive** in Edge Hill is named after the family's main residence, Chatsworth House in Derbyshire.

A number of streets of Kensington are named after Lord Chancellors and Lord Chief Justices of Victorian times. **Denman Street,** as well as **Denman Drive** and **Denman Road** in Newsham Park are named after Lord Chief Justice Thomas Denman. **Coleridge Street** remembers another Lord Chief Justice, while two Lord Chancellors, Lord Cottenham and Lord Halsbury have given their names to **Cottenham Street** and **Halsbury Road**. These streets were so named due to their proximity to the judges lodging in Newsham Park, where the travelling assizes judges would reside while sitting in Liverpool

More recently, wartime Premier Winston Churchill has been commemorated with **Churchill Way North & South**, the two flyovers which connect Commutation Row with Dale Street and Great Crosshall Street in the city centre. No local developer yet has dared name a street after Margaret Thatcher, the longest serving Prime Minister of the 20th century who made few friends on Merseyside. Neither has John Major or Tony Blair been commemorated. However, development by the Labour Council in the 1980's in Vauxhall did lead to a **Callaghan Close**, named after James Callaghan, Prime Minister from 1976 to 1979. When the street was developed, he was the most recent Labour Prime Minister and he is currently the most recent Prime Minister to be remembered in a Liverpool street.

# ROYAL LIVERPOOL

Just as with politicians, earlier royals tend to be commemorated in central Liverpool while later ones are remembered elsewhere. The number of streets that a monarch had named after them is not necessarily in correlation to the number of years spent on the throne, as factors such as extent of development and popularity may have played a part.

The first monarch to be referred to in a street name in Liverpool was Queen Anne, who was on the throne from 1702-14. She gave her name to Queen Street, off Old Hall Street, although this is no longer in existence. However her husband, Prince George of Denmark's name lives on with **George Street** having been named after him. Both these streets were in existence on the first proper map of Liverpool, which was produced in 1725.[18] There is also a **Queen Anne Street** off St Anne Street, which was developed at the end of the eighteenth century.

George I, who reigned from 1714 to 1727, was the first Hanoverian[19] King of Britain. He never learnt the English language and usually conversed with his cabinet ministers in French. Frequent visits to Hanover meant he endeared himself little to the British public and as a consequence there are no streets in Liverpool named after him. His son George II, ruled from 1727 to 1760 and was the last British king to lead troops into battle, albeit Hanoverian ones in the War of the Austrian Succession. Despite his long reign there are no streets named after him, but both his sons are remembered. His younger son, William Duke of Cumberland, gave a Royal Inspection to Liverpool troops in 1746 after they helped defend Carlisle the year before during a Scottish rebellion. To commemorate this, **Hanover Street** was named after the ruling family's surname, while the old 'road to the quarry' became **Duke Street**. In addition to these two streets **Cumberland Street**, off Dale Street, was developed. George II's eldest son was Frederick Lewis, Prince of Wales, who is remembered by **Upper Frederick Street**. He died in 1751 while his father was still alive meaning he never became king and his son George took over as heir to the throne.

George III reigned for sixty years, from 1760 to 1820. This coincided with Liverpool's rapid increase in development, which is reflected by

[18] Produced by J Chadwick.
[19] Hanovarian - line of the House of Hanover.

48

the number of newly laid out streets that were named in his honour, making him by far the most represented sovereign in the city centre. With George Street already in existence, a fitting prefix was added when **Great George Street** was named, as his reign included several significant military victories. Initially called Great George's Street in the 1780s, it was joined by **Great George Place**. Around the time Great George Street was laid out, **Great Charlotte Street** and **Queen Square** were developed to commemorate his queen, Charlotte of Mecklenburg-Strelitz.

There are two squares in different parts of the city centre named in connection with the king. **Great George Square** in Chinatown was meant to house an equestrian statue to commemorate his Golden Jubilee in 1810, but this project was cancelled due to lack of funds. Eventually, the statue was sited in **Monument Place**, the pedestrian area off London Road fronting T J Hughes. As the docks system grew, George's (1771), Kings (1788) and Queens (1800) Docks all honoured George and Charlotte.[20]    These have given rise to the current road names of **George's Dock Gates, Kings Parade, Kings Dock Road** and **Queens Wharf**.

Three of George III's seven children are commemorated in different parts of the city centre. **Cambridge Street, Clarence Street** and **York Street** are all named after the respective dukedoms of Adolphus, William (later William IV) and Frederick. Going even further, the extended family is remembered by **Brunswick Street**, after the family of which the Hanover's were a line. George III's nephew Prince William, Duke of Gloucester and commander of the armed forces in Liverpool is remembered by **Gloucester Street**, which was once 400 yards long but is now only recognisable as the entrance to Lime Street Station. Another street named after him is **Prince William Street** in Toxteth.

During the last ten years of his reign George III's mental illness, which he had suffered from for some time, became so severe that his eldest son, the future George IV, acted as Prince Regent. This fact was commemorated in **Regent Road**, commonly known as the 'dock road', as well as **Regent Street. Brunswick Road**, which links Everton Road and Islington, was developed in the early 1800's and named after Caroline of Brunswick, a member of his extended family who George

---

[20] George's Dock was filled in to make way for the Liver Buildings.

had married in 1795. She gained a lot of sympathy from the British public after mistreatment from the new king, which included being denied access to their daughter and refused admission to his coronation in 1821. The queen also gave her name to Brunswick Dock, which is now served by **Brunswick Way**.

George IV was succeeded in 1830 by his brother William, Duke of Clarence, who had already been commemorated by Clarence Street. Despite only being on the throne for seven years, William IV made his mark with **Upper William Street**, an extension of William Street, which is now called Cotton Street. **Adelaide Place** in Everton commemorates his wife Adelaide of Saxe-Meinengen. Also in Everton **Fitzclarence Walk** and **Fitzclarence Way** have replaced an earlier Fitzclarence Street. This was re-named from Clarence Street when Everton was absorbed into Liverpool. The name Fitzclarence was given to the ten illegitimate children William had with actress Dorothea Jordan.

Queen Victoria, niece of William IV came to the throne at the age of eighteen in 1837, but is not greatly represented in the city centre as it had already become too clustered for further development by this time. However, slum clearance in the 1860s did enable the resulting new thoroughfare to be named **Victoria Street**. **Prince Albert Mount**, near Great George Street, remembers her husband Albert of Saxe-Coburg Gotha. His Germanic origins were recognised in the naming of Coburg Dock, which has subsequently given rise to the road of **Coburg Wharf**. Prince Albert also gave his name to Liverpool's first public park, Princes Park, which was opened in 1849. A boulevard style road was laid out to lead to it, which is flanked on either side by **Princes Avenue** and **Princes Road**.

Near to Prince Albert Mount, Victoria's second son Prince Alfred has given his name to **Alfred Mount**. This is a fairly recent development that takes its name from Alfred Street, which ran from Great George Street to the Anglican Cathedral but has now been demolished. Prince Alfred is also remembered in Wavertree, where he visited in 1866. To mark this, Cow Lane was re-named **Prince Alfred Road**, with a row of houses on it being named **Victoria Terrace**. Nearby is the **Victoria Park** private residential estate, where there is a **Victoria Avenue** and an

**Albert Grove**. Albert Grove is off **Frederick Grove**, which commemorates the marriage of Princess Victoria, the first of Victoria and Albert's nine children, to Frederick William, Crown Prince of Prussia. This cluster of streets is rounded off by **Arnold Grove**, which is named after Frieda Arnold, the Queen's dresser. Elsewhere in Wavertree, **Alfred Street**, off Picton Road, remembers Prince Alfred again.

Between Aigburth Road and Sefton Park, there is an **East, South** and **West Albert Road**, while Alexandra of Denmark (1844-1925), who married Victoria's eldest son Albert Edward (later Edward VII), in 1863 is commemorated by **Alexandra Drive**. Connecting Alexandra Drive to Aigburth Road is **Sandringham Drive**, named after Sandringham House in Norfolk, which was bought by Albert Edward in 1860 and was the birthplace of his son, the future George V. Albert Edward and Alexandra were popular figures who took on a lot of public duties after Queen Victoria became very introverted for some time following the death of her husband in 1861

Off West Derby Road in Tuebrook are **Victoria Road** and **Albert Road**, which are joined by some streets named after their residences. **Buckingham Road** is named after Buckingham Palace, which was purchased by the Royal Family in 1761 but did not become the sovereign's principal residence until Victoria acceded to the throne. **Osborne Road** remembers Osborne House, built between 1845 and 1851 by Victoria and Albert as a holiday home. This palace, on the Isle of Wight, is where Victoria died in 1901. Similarly, in Aigburth, Sandringham House is commemorated, this time by **Sandringham Road**, while **Marlborough Road** takes its name from the London royal residence of Marlborough House, which was occupied by Edward VII before he became king. It is now used as offices of the Commonwealth Secretariat. **Windsor Road** is named after Windsor Castle, which was founded by William the Conqueror in the 11th century.

In Orrell Park there are the familiar names of **Albert Drive** and **Victoria Drive**. Nearby, royal residences are again remembered by **Buckingham Road** and **Windsor Road**, as well as **Balmoral Road**, named after Balmoral Castle in Aberdeenshire, purchased by Prince Albert in 1852. Other streets with a royal theme in this area are **Palace**

**Road** and **Regina Road**, Regina being the Latin word for queen. Off Warbreck Moor stands **Eastbourne Road**, which is named after Victoria's favourite holiday resort. Near the Breeze Hill flyover, two more of their children are honoured. **Arthur Street** is named after the couple's third son Arthur (1850-1942), while his sister Helena (1846-1923) was their third daughter, giving her name to **Helena Street**. Other streets around Liverpool to be named with Victorian connections include **Queens Road** in Everton, which was developed while Victoria was on the throne and **Albert Street** in Edge Hill. There is also an **Empress Road** in Cabbage Hall, which recognises Victoria's position as Empress of India.

Perhaps the most interesting of all streets named in relation to Queen Victoria are to be found in a cluster between Hall Lane and Kensington. These streets were laid out after Victoria's Golden Jubilee in 1887 and the theme includes members of her extended family. Victoria is directly commemorated by **Empress Road**, as is the jubilee itself in **Jubilee Drive**. **Albert Edward Road** and **Renfrew Road** remember the heir to the throne, Baron Renfrew being a title given to him under Scottish peerage. **Leopold Road** and **Albany Road** commemorate his brother Leopold, duke of Albany, while **Connaught Road** is named after Prince Arthur, Duke of Connaught. Albert and Victoria's Germanic connections are remembered in **Saxony Road** and **Guelph Street**, with the Guelphs being a family of which they were a branch line. **Battenberg Street** remembers Prince Henry of Battenberg, who married Princess Beatrice, while **Teck Street** is named after Mary of Teck, who married Victoria's grandson George Duke of York in 1893.

One street with connections to Queen Victoria that stands alone is **Frogmore Road**, off Prescot Road, which is named after the Frogmore mausoleum, where Victoria and Albert are buried. This is situated in the grounds surrounding Windsor Castle and although a crypt with nine spaces for each of their children was built, none of them chose to be buried there.

Edward VII, son of Queen Victoria was sixty when he came to the throne and only reigned for nine years. **King Edward Street**, linking Great Howard Street with New Quay was named after him. In Edge Hill and Wavertree, his wife is honoured by two streets both named

**Alexandra Road**. The street in Edge Hill is the sole survivor of a group of streets to honour Alexandra, her homeland having also been commemorated here by the now demolished Copenhagen Road and Denmark Road.

George V reigned from 1910 to 1936. No streets appear to be named after him, but near to Alexandra Road in Wavertree is **Augusta Close**, which is a relatively new development replacing an earlier Augusta Street. This was named after his wife Victoria Mary Augusta, who was more commonly known as Queen Mary and had already been commemorated by Teck Street before she became queen.

**Queens Drive** was developed as Liverpool's second ring road between 1903 and 1912, during which time both Alexandra and Mary were queen. In 1922 Princess Mary, daughter of George V and Queen Mary, married Viscount Lascelles and to honour this event **Lascelles Road** on the Springwood Estate in Allerton was named.

King George VI, who was on the throne from 1936 to 1952, is not commemorated in name by any streets in Liverpool but **Kingsdale Road** and **Queensdale Road** in Mossley Hill were developed during his reign. Queensdale Road refers to Queen Elizabeth, the Queen Mother who celebrated her 100th birthday in 2000 and died in March 2002. It is a sign of changing attitudes towards the Royal Family that no streets within the Liverpool city boundary have been named in relation to Queen Elizabeth II, despite her having reigned for fifty years. However, there have been some streets named after her in Huyton and Widnes.

# MILITARY LIVERPOOL

Famous battles, wars and military leaders have long been a major factor in the naming of streets in Liverpool. The expansion of the city over time can be seen in the fact that, generally speaking, the more central the street, the longer ago the event that named it took place. However, there are some exceptions to this rule.

During the English Civil War (1642-6), Prince Rupert used the village of Everton, which provided a clear vantage point of Liverpool, to launch his attack on the town. Redevelopment has seen that Rupert Lane, Rupert Terrace, Prince Rupert Street, Rupert Hill and Rupert Grove, which were once all in the Village Street vicinity, have long since disappeared. For the last quarter of the 20th century, the only reminder left was the Rupert Lane Recreation Ground, but the newly created **Rupert Drive** has redressed this balance partly of late.

In Walton, some streets around the village centre were named some 300+ years after the Civil War. An act that eventually led to the Civil War was the refusal by some statesmen to pay ship money, a tax levied by King Charles I for the Royal Navy. Two of these, John Hampden and John Pym, are remembered in **Hampden Street** and **Pym Street**. The war was ended in England when Charles I was defeated at Naseby in 1645 and fled to Scotland, giving rise to the name **Naseby Street**. Following the end of the war, the first commoner to rule England was Oliver Cromwell, after whom **Cromwell Street** is named. His son-in-law Henry Ireton, who was a signatory on the king's death warrant, gives his name to **Ireton Street**.

**Sedgemoor Road** in Norris Green is named after the last battle to take place on English soil. This occurred in 1685 at Sedgemoor in Somerset when James Scott, Duke of Monmouth and illegitimate son of Charles II tried to claim the Crown after the death of his father. Forces representing his uncle, James II, who Charles had nominated to be King before he died, defeated him. In the battle Monmouth was captured and he was later executed for treason.

In 1692 Admiral Edward Russell was in charge of a combined British and Dutch fleet, which defeated a French invasion fleet at the bay of La

Hogue on the north French coast. **Russell Street** in the city centre remembers him.

The War of the Spanish Succession (1701-14) was fought by England, Austria, Netherlands and Denmark against France and Spain. Commander in Chief of the English forces was John Churchill and his victory against the French at Blenheim in 1704 saw the beginning of the decline of French dominance in Europe. Further victories at Ramillies in 1706 and Oudenarde in 1708 saw him given the title 1st Duke of Marlborough. He gives his name to **Marlborough Street**, although this was not named until the end of the 18th century, some time after his victories. Off Penny Lane in Wavertree, two of his victories are remembered by **Blenheim Road** and **Ramillies Road**, both developed in the 20th century. James Butler, 2nd Duke of Ormond (1665-1745), succeeded Marlborough as Commander in Chief of the British forces in 1711, having already served Queen Anne as Lord Lieutenant of Ireland. He was remembered by **Ormond Street**, which is situated off Old Hall Street.

In 1715 John Campbell, 2nd Duke of Argyll, suppressed a Scottish rebellion. He had fought under Marlborough at Malplaquet in 1709 and also played a key part in the opening of negotiations for the Union of England and Scotland, which took place in 1707. **Argyle Street**, which runs parallel to the bottom of Duke Street off Paradise Street, is named after him.

The last British king to participate in battle was George II, at Dettingen, Bavaria in 1743. George, who was also Elector of Hanover, subordinated British interests to take part in the War of the Austrian Succession (1740-8), against an alliance that included France, Prussia and Spain. **Anson Place** and **Anson Street** are named after Admiral George Anson, who was made a Baronet after defeating the French at Cape Finisterre in 1747. During the first four years of the war, he circumnavigated the globe preying on Spanish colonies and ships, bringing back a fortune in treasure. This war also has the distinction of giving name to the only street in Liverpool that commemorates a defeat. **Fontenoy Street** remembers a 1745 loss in the Battle of Fontenoy in Belgium, when the French beat British, Austrian and Dutch forces.

The Seven Years War of 1756-63 saw Britain line up alongside Hanover and Prussia against Austria, France, Russia, Spain and Sweden for control of Germany and colonial supremacy in North America and India. The Prussian alliance was commemorated by **Prussia Street**, which once ran from Old Hall Street to Pall Mall and beyond but was cut in two by the building of Exchange Station, now Mercury Court office buildings. Admiral Edward Hawke, after whom **Hawke Street** is named, won the Battle of Quiberon Bay off the coast of Brittany in 1759, thwarting a planned French invasion of England. James Wolfe was Britain's second in command in North America and gives his name to **Wolfe Street** in Toxteth. He was killed in battle while taking Quebec from the French in 1759.

Three years after the Seven Years War ended, in 1766, a French invasion was threatened. Gill Slater commanded the Liverpool Volunteers,[21] which was raised in response to this and **Slater Street** and **Slater Place** remember him. Another local man who would raise an army at his own expense was Colonel John Bolton, who gathered 800 locals in 1797 when the French tried to invade Wales. Bolton lived in Duke Street and in 1805 he won the last duel to be fought in Liverpool. Although charged with murder, he was saved by the weight of public opinion in his favour and never stood trial. He is honoured in Liverpool by **Bolton Street**, near Lime Street.

During the last third of the 18th century a number of colonial battles were fought as Britain held on to colonies and fought off the threat of other powers that tried to exert a naval influence. In 1782, French hopes for supremacy in the West Indies were ended by a three day battle off Dominica. Under the command of Admiral George Brydges, the French commander François de Grasse was captured along with seven of his ships. Brydges was given the title of 1st Baron Rodney for this victory and in Liverpool the proposed name for Schlink Street, after a Dutch local landowner, was changed to **Rodney Street**. On his return to England, Rodney was a champion of the slave trade and spoke against its abolition in the House of Lords. Another Rodney Street was developed in Toxteth, but to avoid confusion this was later changed to its present title of **Admiral Street,** with an **Admiral Grove** also being present nearby. He is also commemorated by **Brydges Street** in Edge Hill.

---

[21] Citizens regiment of volunteer soldiers.

Britain had taken possession of the rock of Gibraltar in 1704, during the War of the Spanish Succession. When Spain entered the War of American Independence against the British it laid siege to the colony from 1779 to 1783, only ending it when peace preliminaries were signed. **Gibraltar Row** commemorates this and there was once a Gibraltar Street. **Elliot Street**, near Clayton Square, is named after George Augustus Elliot, one of the British defenders of the siege.

The threat of Dutch naval superiority over Britain was ended in 1797 by victory over Admiral de Winter at Camperdown, off the Dutch coast. Under the command of Admiral Adam Duncan, the Dutch fleet was destroyed and **Duncan Street** was named in his honour. Also in 1797 the French fleet were defeated at Cape St Vincent, off Portugal. The commander, Admiral John Jervis (1735-1823) was made 1st Earl of St. Vincent and **St. Vincent Street** was laid out in the early 19th century. **St. Vincent Way**, developed later, is also present.

The Napoleonic Wars, fought between France and a number of European powers from 1799 to 1815 saw a number of significant military victories on land and sea. The main naval hero of the wars was Horatio Nelson, who was already a distinguished commander, having won earlier battles against the French before key victories at Copenhagen in 1801 and Trafalgar in 1805. At Copenhagen he destroyed the Danish fleet, which was giving economic aid to France. Already having lost an eye and arm in battle, he was then mortally wounded at Trafalgar in a victory that put paid to French leader Napoleon's planned invasion of England. In the city centre, **Nelson Street** and **Lord Nelson Street** are both named after him. His Flag Captain, Lieutenant Thomas Masterman Hardy (1769-1839) is remembered by **Hardy Street**, which runs parallel to Nelson Street. Hardy commanded HMS Victory at Trafalgar and was at Nelson's side as he died. Off Brunswick Road, **Trafalgar Way** remembers Nelson's final battle.

Admiral William Hotham (1736-1813) and Admiral Alexander Hood, Lord Bridport (1726-1814) both commanded Nelson in his earlier years in the navy. **Hotham Street**, which was originally called Duncan Street and linked Copperas Hill with London Road, is named in Hotham's honour. The street was considerably reduced by the expansion of Lime

Street station and the tiny section left at the Copperas Hill end is now **Hotham Place**. Off Hotham Street is **Bridport Street**, which remembers Hood. He served in the navy for 54 years, still commanding at the age of 74.

A less famous commander than Nelson was Admiral James Gambier. Before being out in charge of the Channel fleet from 1808 to 1811 he was involved in a bombardment of Copenhagen in 1807. His actions in the Napoleonic Wars led to him being appointed Governor of Newfoundland in Canada. In Liverpool **Gambier Terrace**, which was developed in the 1830s and overlooks the Anglican Cathedral, honours him. When Napoleon was transported to exile at St. Helena in 1815 the commander of the ship that carried him was Sir George Cockburn (1772-1853). He had served under Nelson in the Mediterranean from 1795 to 1797 and is remembered in Toxteth by **Cockburn Street**.

The Napoleonic wars eventually ended in 1815 when Napoleon was defeated in the land Battle of Waterloo in Belgium, an event that was commemorated when **Waterloo Road** was developed. The battle also gave the name to Waterloo Dock and the road around it, **Waterloo Quay**. There is also a **Waterloo Street** in Wavertree. Arthur Wellesley, Duke of Wellington was in command of the Allied armies at Waterloo, but considering how successful he was in military terms, **Wellington Street**, north of the city centre is very low key. Throughout the city however, he has more streets named after him than any other military figure, of which **Wellington Road** in Wavertree is a main route. There is another **Wellington Road** in Toxteth, where **Wellesley Road** and **Wellesley Terrace** remember his real surname.

It was not just Europe where Napoleon was fought. Sir Ralph Abercromby (1734-1801), after whom **Abercromby Square** is named, was killed in the Battle of Alexandria, which saw the Egyptian city given back to the Turks following a British attack on the occupying French forces.

Although there were many important victories during George III's reign, it was not always successful, as he ruled over Britain's loss of America as a colony during the American War of Independence (1775-83). **Cornwallis Street** is named after Charles Cornwallis, whose surrender at Yorktown in 1781 helped ensure American victory. However, despite this defeat, he would later, negotiate the Treaty of Amiens in 1802 that ended one phase of the Napoleonic Wars.

By the mid 19th century, most of the main streets in the city centre as we know it today were in place, meaning later military campaigns were remembered further afield. For instance, the Crimean War, which was fought between Britain, France and Turkey against Russia between 1853 and 1856, is commemorated in Garston, Aigburth and Wavertree. **Raglan Street** and **Raglan Walk** in Garston are named after Fitzroy James Henry Somerset, 1st Baron Raglan. He was an aide-de-camp[22] to the Duke of Wellington at Waterloo, before going on to command British forces in Crimea where he died of dysentery. A key victory in the Crimean War was the battle for the Alma River and **Alma Road** in Aigburth and **Alma Terrace** in Wavertree remember this. Also in Wavertree there is a **Cambridge Street,** named after George William Frederick Charles, 2nd Duke of Cambridge, who was a commander in Crimea. He was a grandson of George III.

A gun made at the Fawcett Preston foundry of Duke Street fired the first shot of the American Civil War (1861-5). Initially this was called the Phoenix Foundry and **Lydia Ann Street**, which led to it, was named after the wife of its founder George Perry.

In 1867 Thoedore II of Abyssinia (now Ethiopia) imprisoned the British consul and other Europeans after Britain rebuked his efforts to form an alliance. An invasion force was sent and the fall of the fortress of Magdala led to Theodore committing suicide rather than face capture. **Magdala Street** in Toxteth commemorates this, while **Abyssinia Close** in Wavertree, which has replaced an earlier Abyssinia Street, remembers the campaign as a whole.

A **Bosnia Street** exists in Toxteth, although it has not been named in relation to events of the 1990s. This street was in existence over 100 years earlier following the Congress of Berlin in 1878, which saw the ex Turkish province of Bosnia mandated to Austria-Hungary following Russia's victory over the Turks. Britain was a major player in the Congress, due to its concern over Russia's growing military strength.

---

[22] Aide-de-camp - officer who gives general secretarial and administrative support.

There used to be a Balkan Street and a Plevna street, named after the city whose fall led to Turkish calls for an armistice, but these two streets have now been swept away by redevelopment.

In Fazakerley, a number of streets are linked to the Boer War of 1899-1902, which was fought in South Africa between British forces and Dutch settlers. **Ladysmith Road** is named after the siege of the railway town of Ladysmith, while **Delagoa Road** is named after Delagoa Bay, an important seaport during the war. The town of Harrismith was a major British base and is remembered by **Harrismith Road. Cape Road** and **Natal Road** are named after Britain's two colonies involved and **Pretoria Road** is named after a Boer capital that was captured by the British. **Redvers Drive** and **Kitchener Drive** in Orrell Park are named after Boer War commanders Sir Redvers Buller and Horatio Kitchener.

Some more streets in Fazakerely are associated with the 1st World War. **Karonga Road** is named after the site of a battle in Malawi that was fought against forces from German East Africa. **Manica Crescent** remembers HMS Manica, a kite balloon ship that was used at Gallipoli, when allied forces unsuccessfully tried to invade Turkey to re-take Istanbul.

The 1st World War is also commemorated by a small cluster of streets off St Oswald's Street in Old Swan. **Allenby Square** is named after Edward Allenby who led the offensive against the Turks, capturing Damascus and Jerusalem, while **Rawlinson Road** commemorates Sir Henry Rawlinson, who played a major role in the Battle of the Somme. A naval commander, David Beatty is remembered by **Beatty Road**. He played a part in the Battle of Jutland in 1916, when the Allied naval blockade of Germany was maintained, despite the German fleet being of greater numbers. Not far from here, off Edge Lane Drive, is **Sturdee Road**, named after Admiral Sir Charles Doveton Sturdee, whose victory in the Battle of the Falklands in 1914 gave Britain control of the ocean trade routes.

In 1995, to commemorate the 50th anniversary of the Battle of the Atlantic, which was fought from 1940 to 1944, **Canada Boulevard** was created in front of the three main waterfront buildings. This was named to honour Canada's involvement in the naval battle, which was co-ordinated from Liverpool, while **Roosevelt Drive** in Aintree remembers American 2nd World War president Franklin D. Roosevelt. As with royalty, more recent conflicts have not been remembered within the city boundary. This is despite the large-scale building programmes that went on in the 1950s, which for whatever reason have failed to recognise the 2nd World War. The nearest large scale of World War Two linked streets is in Huyton.

# LIVERPOOL'S LUNGS
# BOTANICAL GARDENS & 19TH CENTURY PARKS

During the late 19th century it became apparent that Liverpool's residents needed somewhere they could go to escape the increasing overcrowding and pollution in the town. The answer lay in the botanical gardens and parks, which provided an oasis of calm for town dwellers and in the case of botanical gardens, the opportunity to see plants that were native to other lands.

The first botanical gardens were opened in 1802 in Olive Street, which was situated off Crown Street. As the built up area encroached on these gardens in the next few decades, many of the newly laid out streets were named with a botanical theme and remain in existence today. Major routes are **Grove Street** and **Myrtle Street**, the myrtle being a tree/shrub found in tropical America and Asia. Another street named after a plant from the Tropics is **Mulberry Street**, while **Peach Street** and **Walnut Street** have just about survived total obliteration by the University of Liverpool, remaining as pedestrian throughways in the campus.

The botanical gardens remained in Grove Street until 1836, when the expanding town meant it was necessary for them to move to a site off Edge Lane, which was then out in the country. The land south of the new gardens was originally meant to be a gaol, but when this idea was deemed impractical it was developed into Wavertree Park in 1856. This is now known as Botanic Park and the original site of the walled gardens is still intact and in use as part of the park. **Botanic Road**, which runs alongside the park, was named in honour of the gardens. Terraced property began to engulf this area in the 1860s and a number of new roads laid out between Edge Lane and Prescot Road continued the naming precedent set by streets around the first gardens in the city centre. These included **Laburnum Road, Laurel Road** and **Lilley Road**.

Today, the botanical gardens are situated in Calderstones Park, one of several public parks in the city. It was realised in the 19th century that there was a need for open spaces where residents could exercise because, although there was St James Walk on the site of the Anglican Cathedral, this was still near to the fumes from the docks. Princes Park was the first public park to be developed in 1849 and in the 1860s the corporation decided to build three large parks in the south, middle and north of the city. These were Sefton Park, Newsham Park and Stanley Park. The parks that were built gave rise to a number of streets which have been covered elsewhere in this book, but there are some unique names that can only be featured here.

Around the perimeter of Princes Park, land was sold for the building of upper class residences so that the development costs of the park could be recouped in ground rent. One of the roads developed was **Belvidere Road**, which was named as a compliment to the Classical style of the houses, a belvedere being a detached structure built to command a view. The word comes from two Italian words meaning beautiful and to see. Interestingly, it is actually mis-spelled; Belvedere, as in the school, is the correct way.

**Ullett Road** separates Princes Park from the much larger Sefton Park. This name derives from owlet and the section between Sefton Park Road and Smithdown Road was in existence in the 18th century as Owlet Lane. Two roads, **Livingston Drive North** and **Livingston Drive South** were laid out to connect Sefton Park with Lark Lane and Aigburth Road respectively. They were named after Joseph G. Livingston, from whom the land was bought to provide the approaches.

In Newsham Park there is an **Orphan Drive**. This was named after the Royal Liverpool Seamen's Orphan Institution, which was in existence from 1864 to 1949 in the building that is now Park Hospital.

Throughout Liverpool, there are reminders of greener pastures in the names of many streets. Builders may have been hoping residents would re-create a rural air in their imagination, but an article in the *Liverpool Citizen* of 1890 suggested that some of these should be renamed, as they did nothing to reflect their surroundings. The writer may have been referring to **Moss Grove** and **Fern Grove** in Toxteth, or **Crocus Street** and **Snowdrop Street** in Kirkdale, which were far from the countryside when developed. The names have survived however and there are many more modern developments that have continued to give rise to botanical names. One example is **Lavender Way**, near Walton Park. Roads off this are **Buttercup Way, Dahlia Close, Honeysuckle Drive** and **Limetree Close.** In Croxteth Park, **Fir Tree Drive** rings the estate, which includes roads such as **Elm Close, The Cedars** and **The Oaks**.

# THE WELSH & SCOTTISH INFLUENCE

The Welsh and Scottish influence in Liverpool can be seen by a number of streets around the city, although the Welsh were more prominent. Streets developed by builders would often remember their homelands and in some cases leave residents quite tongue twisted!

In the mid to late 19th century, there were a number of Welsh building societies, estate agents and builders in Liverpool. One famous builder was John Jones, nicknamed 'Drinkwater' because of his refusal to pay workmen the customary price of a pint of beer when the first house in a terrace was completed. Another was William Jones, the first Welsh-speaking mayor of Bootle who built streets in Everton and Toxteth.

Off High Park Street in Toxteth, **Dovey Street, Elwy Street** and **Gwydir Street** are all named after Welsh rivers, with Kinmel Bay giving its name to **Kinmel Street**. **Madryn Street** and **Powis Street** are named after castles in Gwynedd and Powys respectively, although Madryn Castle was demolished in 1968 and is now a caravan park. **Pengwern Street, Rhiwlas Street** and **Wynnstay Street** take their names from villages while **Voelas Street** is named after a country house estate in the Vale of Conwy. **Teilo Street** is named after a 6th century Welsh saint who allegedly accompanied St. David on a pilgrimage to Jerusalem. A smaller number of Welsh streets can be found on the other side of Park Road, off Park Street. Here, **Rhyl Street** is named after the north Welsh coastal resort, while **Llanwryst Close** has replaced the earlier Llanwryst Street. This was named after the town of Llanwryst, which like the Voelas Estate is in the Vale of Conwy.

In Vauxhall, around the Athol Street and Boundary Street area, a number of terraced streets were developed with Welsh connections. Most of these have been cleared, but some street names do survive. Amongst those still present are **Denbigh Street** and **Milford Street**, which are named after towns. **Barmouth Way** and **Newport Court** are both newly created, using names from streets that were first developed years before. Extensive re-development has occurred around Breck Road and Everton Road, but a Welsh name that lives on is **Aber Street**, named after a village near Bangor. **Fishguard Close** remembers an earlier street that was named after a port in south west Wales, while

**Lavan Street** and the newer **Lavan Close** are named after the Lavan Sands in north west Wales.

Off Walton Breck Road, a Free Welsh Church was established at the corner of Donaldson Street and Glaisher Street, which still stands as Crete Hall. In the immediate vicinity is **Tenby Street**, which is named after a town in south Wales. Nearby is **Vrynwy Street**, which takes its name from Lake Vrynwy, Liverpool's main water supply since the 1880s when a reservoir was constructed there. Off Oakfield Road, **Bala Street** is also named after a lake, while **Dinorwic Road** and **Valley Road** are named after villages in Gwynedd and Anglesey respectively. **Skerries Road** takes its name from a small group of uninhabited islands off the northwestern Anglesey coast. Amongst these streets named after Welsh places are a number which were given girls names. They are **Wylva Road, Edith Road, Miriam Road, Gertrude Road, Elsie Road** and **Lilian Road**. It may be that they were names of family members of the builder. One street on the edge of the city centre that definitely was named after family connections was **Catherine Street**. This was developed and lived in by Welshman William Jones and named after his mother.

A family firm of builders, 'Owen and William Owen Elias', who were father and son, built streets in Walton that spelt out the name of their firm in alphabetical order. Between County Road and Goodison Road, running in this order are **O**wen, **W**inslow, **E**ton, **N**eston, **A**ndrew, **N**imrod, **D**ane, **W**ilburn, **I**smay, **L**ind, **L**owell, **I**ndex and **A**rnot Streets. The sequence continues on the other side of County road with **M**akin, **O**lney, **W**eldon, **E**uston and **N**ixon Streets. Over Bedford Road, the sequence is reversed to complete the title, with **E**lton, **L**iston, **I**mrie and **A**stor Streets being joined slightly further along by Stuart Road, the only one of the sequence not directly next to its predecessor. In between Goodison Road and City Road, a third generation of the family is commemorated. William's son E. Alfred has his name spelt out by **E**spin, **A**skew, **L**inton, **F**rodsham, **R**ipon, **E**mery and **D**yson Streets. This Welsh dynasty had been started in Everton by Owen Elias (1806-80), who built a lot of terraced property on the slopes between Great Homer Street and Netherfield Road North. He named one of these, Elias Street after himself although this is no longer in existence.

Not all streets in Liverpool with Welsh connections were necessarily named by Welsh builders. More recently developed, near the junction of West Derby Road and Belmont Road are **Conwy Drive, Gwent Close, Cardigan Way** and **Montgomery Way**. These are the results of clearance of terraced streets and the only Welsh influence before this in the area was **Celt Street**, which is now considerably shorter than before due to the recreation ground. There is a newly built **Clwyd Grove** in West Derby, while in the southern end of the city new developments off Riverside Drive have led to the creation of **Moel Famau View**. This is named after the 555 metre high mountain in the Clwydian hills, which can be seen from the vicinity on a clear day.

Although not as prominent as the Welsh builders, the Scots did have an influence in the rise of Liverpool. In the city centre, there was a considerable Scottish presence in the Rodney Street area from the beginning of the 19th century. St Andrew's Church was built, as was the Caledonian School and **Caledonia Street** remembers their presence here. Nearby **Melville Place** is named after Viscount Melville, an 18th century politician who was known as 'the uncrowned King of Scotland'.

There are some clusters of streets around Edge Lane and Prescot Road that hint at a Scottish influence when they were built. In Fairfield **Balmoral Road, Carstairs Road, Huntly Road** and **Kelso Road** are all named after Scottish towns. In the nearby Stanley district, **Cheviot Road** and **Grampian Road** are named after mountain ranges, while **Lomond Road** commemorates one of Scotland's highest mountains. **Clyde Road** takes its name from the river that runs through Glasgow and the water theme continues with **Lorne Street**, named after the Firth of Lorne on the west coast. Scottish towns are remembered here in **Barrymore Road, Dunmore Road, Glencairn Road** and **Selkirk Road**. Nearer to the city centre, off West Derby Road a Scot built **Dunkeld Street** and **Perth Street** in the 1860s.

# LOCAL RELIGIOUS FIGURES AND CHURCHES

In Liverpool city centre there are many reminders of bygone churches and figures associated with them. Citywide, many streets have also been influenced by places of worship, with a number of Church Streets and Church Roads being in existence.

Liverpool's main shopping street, **Church Street** takes its name from St Peters Church, which was built after Liverpool became a parish in its own right in 1699. The church was demolished in1922 and also gave its name to **Church Alley**, which ran alongside it. An un-named track to the rear of the church was first named Peter Street by 1766. In the late 18th century the name was changed to its current **Peters Lane** when another Peter Street came into existence off Whitechapel. Off Church Street is **Basnett Street**, laid out on land owned by the Basnett family in the mid 18th century. One member of the family, Christopher Basnett, was the first minister of the Key Street Presbyterian Chapel, which stood off Tithebarn Street on the site of the Mercury Court office complex.

At the rear of St. George's Hall lie St. Johns Gardens, which opened in 1904 after the demolition of St. Johns Church. The church had been built around 1770 and **St Johns Lane** took its name from it, having once been known as Fall Well Lane. The original name had come from the fact it led to the Fall Well, which stood in the vicinity and was Liverpool's main water supply. Another place of worship long demolished is the ancient Chapel of St. Mary Del Key, which in addition to giving its name to one of the original seven streets, Chapel Street, is now commemorated by **Old Churchyard**. This was originally called Chapel Yard in the early 18th century. As land was reclaimed to build Liverpool's docks, the old chapels successor has not been forgotten as **St. Nicholas Place** leads to the landing stage.

The first enclosed garden built in Liverpool was **Wostenholme Square**, developed in the mid 18th century as a select locality on land on which the Reverend M. Wostenholme resided. In Chinatown, **Raffles Street** is named after another Reverend, Thomas Stamford Raffles. He was a minister of Great George Street Congregational Chapel, now the 'Blackie' arts centre.

In the 1850s Holy Cross Church was built in Great Crosshall Street. This was named after St. Patricks Cross, which stood nearby at the junction of Marybone, Tithebarn Street and Vauxhall Road until the late 18th Century. The cross is commemorated by a plaque in a memorial garden next to the church, created after it closed in 2002. **Holy Cross Close**, off Addison Street, was developed in the late 20th century. Next to this is **St. Stephen's Place**, developed at the same time. This is named after an earlier St. Stephen's Street, which had commemorated a church of the same name that stood on Byrom Street. Saint Stephen was the first Christian Martyr, stoned to death around AD36 in Jerusalem. Tucked away off Dale Street, **Quakers Alley** takes its name from an 18th century Friends Meeting House and burial ground. This stood on the corner with Hackins Hey and had been set up by the Religious Society of Friends, more commonly known as Quakers. They see divine revelation as immediate and individual.

As slum properties began to engulf Old Hall Street in the late 18th century, many merchants moved out towards Everton, around **St. Anne Street**. This was named after St Anne's Church, which was built in 1772 and named after the mother of the Virgin Mary. Another church built around this time as development took place away from the centre was St. James Church in Toxteth, which gives its name to **St. James Street** and **St. James Place**. The former was part of the old Park Lane but a section of it was re-named after the church was built.

On the corner of Myrtle Street and Hope Street stood the Myrtle Street Baptist Church, now the site of Liverpool Community College. A minister of this was Hugh Stowell Brown, who gives his name to nearby **Stowell Street**. He administered charity locally and set up a savings bank for his parishioners. Further up Myrtle Street was Holy Innocents Church, which stood on the site of **Minster Court**. This name was arrived at in the early 1990s, having earlier been Myrtle Gardens and Minster Gardens. Near to the corner of Canning Street and Catherine Street is St. Brides Church, named after St Bride (or St. Brigid), one of the three patron saints of Ireland. She was a fifth century nun who founded four monasteries and the church has given its name to **St. Bride Street**.

Canon T. Major Lester (1829-1903) was a vicar in Kirkdale for fifty years. He founded the Walton School Board in 1863 and built Major Lester School in 1860. This was financed from begging letters and he also helped to found hospitals. **Major Street** and **Lester Close** in Kirkdale take their names from him. For nearly 80 years, between 1768 and 1847, father and son Henry and Samuel Heathcote were rectors of St. Mary's Church in Walton and **Heathcote Road** remembers them. The church itself has given its name to **St Mary's Avenue, Grove, Place** and **Lane**.

Although not all of them still stand today, some Catholic churches in the Scotland Road area are remembered by street names. **Silvester Street** took its name from St. Silvesters Church, which was named after St Silvester, Pope from 314-335. On the other side of Scotland Road is St Anthony's Church, which gives its name to **St. Anthony's Place**. Three new streets have been named since the 1980s. St Joseph's Church stood in Grosvenor Street and is remembered today by **St. Joseph's Crescent**, while another church, St Albans in Denbigh Street gave its name to **St. Albans Court**. A former Catholic Archbishop of Liverpool who held the post from 1894 to 1921 was Thomas Whiteside,[23] is remembered by **Whiteside Close**.

In West Derby, the Christopher Grange Blind Institute was opened in 1972. This was founded as long ago as 1841 as the Catholic Blind Asylum in Islington. The original founder, The Very Reverend Doctor Thomas Youens is remembered by **Youens Way**, which connects the institute to East Prescot Road. Youens was rector of St Nicholas pro cathedral in Copperas Hill and noted in Liverpool for his work with poor people, especially his vast interest in the blind.

St. Oswald's Catholic Church in Old Swan was founded in 1842 and gives its name to **St. Oswald's Street**, which was once part of Edge Lane. Off this is **Maddocks Street**, which is named after Canon Maddocks, the first priest in the church. This was the first street in Liverpool to be named after a local Catholic churchman and remained the only one until Whiteside Close was developed over 100 years later. Also in the Old Swan/Stoneycroft area stand three Russian named streets. They were named after evangelist Heber Radcliffe, who owned land locally and went on a mission to Russia. As a surprise for him on

---

[23] Not given title of Archbishop until 1911.

his return, the long roads of **Kremlin Drive, Moscow Drive** and **Russian Drive** were laid out, with the latter two being linked by the smaller **Russian Avenue**. Nearby, **Brookland Road East** and **Brookland Road West** are named after a former rector of Liverpool, Archdeacon Brooks, who owned the land on which it was built. It had been acquired by his ancestor Joseph Brooks in 1782.

In Wavertree, **Church Road** and **Church Road North** were created by the Wavertree Enclosure Act of 1768, which allowed for the division of land into fields. The initially unnamed lanes were later formally named after Holy Trinity Church, which dates from 1794. Staying in Wavertree, St. Mary's Church in Victoria Park was built in 1837 and replaced a Wesleyan Methodist Chapel that is now remembered by **Wesley Place**.

Near to Otterspool, a Puritan settlement developed in the 17th century known as 'Little Jordan'. This was sited next to the River Jordan, which is now mainly culverted. Jericho Farm was set up and this was connected to Aigburth Road (then Park Lane) by an un-named lane that became **Jericho Lane**. The farmhouse was demolished in 1960 but **Jericho Farm Close** was developed and named after the settlement. Monks from Stanlawe Abbey in Cheshire once owned Land in Garston. Some streets in this area are named in relation to this, including **Priory Street**, which takes its name from a religious house that monks live in. **Monkfield Way** is named after an area known as the Monks Field, situated where the railway line forks to go down to the docks.

In Woolton Village there is a **James Road** and **James Court**. These are named after the St. James Wesleyan Methodist and United Reform Church at the bottom of **Church Road South**, which along with **Church Road** is named after the Church of St. Peters, completed in 1826. **St. Mary's Street** in Woolton takes its name from St. Mary's Church, which was built in 1860 due to the growing influx of Irish Catholics in the vicinity as St. Benet's Priory in Watergate Lane was by then inadequate. St. Stephen's Church in Belle Vale has been responsible for the naming of **Churchfield Road, St Stephens Close** and **Vicarage Lawn**.

When the Eldonian Village was built in the 1980s, Liverpool's two leading churchmen at the time were commemorated. **Archbishop**

**Worlock Court** is named after the Roman Catholic Archbishop of Liverpool, Derek Worlock, who died in 1996 after serving the city for twenty years. The Anglican bishop, the Right Reverend David Sheppard was remembered by **Bishop Sheppard Court**. Sheppard, who held the position for 22 years, had earlier played cricket for 15 years for Sussex, as well as captaining England for a short time. They jointly published a book, *Better Together*, the title of which was borrowed from the Eldonians motto: 'We Do It Better Together'. In the 1990s, development has taken place on land fronting the Anglican Cathedral, with **Dean Dillistone Court** and **Dean Patey Court** both remembering former deans. To mark the new millennium an environmentally friendly development was built at the back of the Church of the Good Shepherd in Croxteth. **Good Shepherd Close** was developed by Riverside Housing in 1999 and contains solar panels and low flush lavatories, amongst other things.

# WIDER RELIGIOUS INFLUENCES

Throughout Liverpool there are a number of streets named after biblical characters, religious figures or cathedrals. Most of these streets were developed during the 19th and early 20th centuries, although some have only been named in the past decade or so.

Perhaps the most well known of Liverpool's religious streets are in an area known as the Holyland in Toxteth. This is situated between Beresford Road, Mill Street, Park Road and Park Hill Road and its nickname comes from the biblical names given to the streets. **Moses Street** is named after the Hebrew prophet who was founder of the Jewish people, while **David Street** commemorates the King of Judea and Israel who founded Jerusalem as the nations capital. **Isaac Street** is name after Isaac, father of Jacob, whose twelve sons became the patriarchs of the twelve tribes of Israel, while Jacob himself is remembered in **Jacob Street**. Running across all four streets is **Grace Street**, which in Christian theology is a term meaning unearned favour bestowed on people by God.

Off Northumberland Street in Toxteth is **Doddridge Street**, which is named after Philip Doddridge (1702-51), a non-conformist hymn writer who wrote *The Rise and Progress Of Religion in the Soul*. At the end of Doddridge Road is **Tillotson Close**, named after a 17th century Archbishop of Canterbury, John Tillotson. In the Granby area of Toxteth, **Kingsley Road** is named after Charles Kingsley, an Anglican priest who was known for his liberal views. He also taught history at Cambridge in the 1860s and his novels displayed sympathy with the economically depressed classes of his day.

In between Scotland Road and Vauxhall Road, a leading figure of the English Reformation, Thomas Cranmer (1489-1556) is remembered in **Cranmer Street**. As Archbishop of Canterbury under Henry VIII, he oversaw the removal of the Pope's name from every prayer book and proclaimed the King the Head of the English Church. However, when Henry's daughter Mary, a Catholic, came to the throne in 1553 Cranmer was arrested for treason and burnt at the stake on 21st March 1556. Someone else who suffered the same fate at the hands of 'Bloody Mary' was Hugh Latimer, after whom **Latimer Street** is named. He was the Bishop of Worcester and burnt on 16th October 1555, one of 300 to be condemned for heresy during her reign. It was an ironic twist of fate that when they were built, it was Irish Catholic immigrants that tended to inhabit these two streets. Around 100 years ago a local councillor tried in vain to have the names changed, even climbing up walls to try and take the signs down.

Two medieval churchmen are remembered in Kirkdale. **Becket Street** is named after Thomas a Becket (c1118-70), the Archbishop of Canterbury who was murdered by four of the King's men, although not on the King's orders. William of Wykeham (1324-1404) gives his name to **Wykeham Street**. He was Bishop of Winchester and father of the English public schools system. Sandwiched between these streets is **Newman Street**, named after John Henry Newman (1801-90), an outstanding religious thinker and essayist who became a cardinal after his conversion to the Catholic Church.

Also in Kirkdale, **Westminster Road** was widened in the 1860s and re-named from Field lane. It is named after Westminster Abbey in London, where English monarchs are crowned and many are buried along with a number of other prominent citizens. Westminster Road leads on to **Lambeth Road**, named after Lambeth Palace in London, the Archbishop of Canterbury's principal residence. Other streets in this area to be named after abbeys are **Fonthill Street, Fonthill Close** and **Furness Street**. Fonthill Abbey is in Wiltshire, while Furness Abbey in Cumbria is now in ruins. Fountains Abbey, near Ripon in Yorkshire is probably Britain's most well-known monastic ruin and is remembered by **Fountains Road** and **Fountains Close**. In Everton, **Spurgeon Close** has replaced an earlier Spurgeon Street. This is named after Charles Haddon Spurgeon (1834-92), a preacher who founded Spurgeon's College in London for the training of men in Christian service.

In Orrell Park, **Renwick Road** remembers American architect James Renwick, who built the Grace Church in New York City as his first major project. The church, which was built in a gothic revival style between 1846 and 1849, gives its name to **Grace Road**. Renwick then went on to design the Smithsonian Institute in Washington DC and Saint Patrick's Cathedral in New York.

Off Townsend Lane in Cabbage Hall a number of streets are named after religious buildings and church positions. **Abbey Road** and **Monastery Road** take their names from communities of monks, **Cathedral Road** from the principal church of a diocese and **Chapel Road** from a place of worship within a church. **Bishop Road** is named after the clergyman in charge of a whole diocese, while **Curate Road** and **Vicar Road** are named after types of local clergymen. **Rector Road** comes from the figure that is the head priest of a religious institution. **Canon Street** could be named either after a member of a cathedral or a church decree. Slightly further down Townsend Lane, **Wycliffe Road** is named after John Wycliffe (1330-84), a philosopher who was a forerunner of the Reformation, believing Christians should have a direct relationship with God without the need for parish priests.

In the first decade of the 20th century, Charles Berrington of Bedford acquired the Heathfield Park Estate in Wavertree and set about development. He named **Charles Berrington Road** after himself, the full name rather than just the surname being used so as to avoid confusion with Barrington Road. His cousin and foreman joiner was named Litchfield and this was corrupted to form **Lichfield Road**. Lichfield is a cathedral city and all the other streets on the state, between Charles Berrington Road and Church Road are named after cathedrals. Amongst these is **Truro Road**, after the first cathedral to be consecrated since the Reformation and **Hereford Road**, after Hereford Cathedral, which has on exhibit a 1290 map of the world portraying Jerusalem as the centre. Other cathedral cities are commemorated in **Beverley Road, Bristol Road, Coventry Road, Newcastle Road, Norwich Road** and **Peterborough Road**.

Cathedral cities are also commemorated by a number of streets in Garston, near to Banks Road. **Lincoln Street** is named after a cathedral on which building commenced in the 11th century, while Durham Cathedral, which was finished in 1133, gives its name to **Durham Street**. Canterbury Cathedral, which was started in the 12th century after an earlier church was destroyed by fire, is remembered by **Canterbury Street** and **York Street** and **York Way** takes their names from York Minster, a cathedral that retains more medieval glass than any other.

Off Bentham Drive and Bowland Avenue in Childwall some saints are commemorated. A 3rd century saint and martyr, St. Alban, was a Roman soldier who converted to Christianity and was be-headed for sheltering a priest. The site of the town where this occurred, Verulanium was later named St. Albans after him, as was **Alban Road**. In the 4th century St. Basil wrote Christian doctrines that are still followed by most Orthodox monks today and **Basil Close** and **Basil Road** remember him. The patron saint of travellers, St. Christopher, of whom there is no documentary evidence of his existence, gives his name to **Christopher Close** and **Christopher Way**. **Dominic Close, Dominic Road** and **Francis Way** remember two founders of Christian orders. St. Dominic was a Spanish theologian who founded the Dominicans, known as the Black Friars in this country, while St. Francis of Assisi was founder of the Franciscan Monks. **Gregory Close** and **Gregory Way** are named after St. Gregory, Pope 590-604 and one of the four doctors of the church.[24]

In addition to the saints in Childwall, two scholars also have streets named after them. **Lanfranc Way** and **Lanfranc Close** are named after Lanfranc, 11th century Italian ecclesiastic who was Archbishop of Canterbury from 1070 to 1089 after being installed by William the Conqueror. Origen, who gives his name to **Origen Road**, was an Egyptian writer and theologian who taught in Palestine, was imprisoned for a year in AD 250 and died three years later, weakened by injuries sustained there.

Nearly all of the streets with religious connections mentioned so far were developed before the 2nd World War, but more recently there have been streets with this theme built in Croxteth Park. **Lindisfarne Drive** remembers the Celtic monastery of Lindisfarne. This was founded in 653 and one of its early priors St. Cuthbert gives his name to **St. Cuthberts Close**. The west Hebridean monastery of Iona, established in the 6th century is commemorated in **Iona Close**, while **Tewkesbury Close** takes its name from an 11th century abbey in Gloucestershire.

---

[24] Eminent Christian teacher who contributed to the understanding of the faith.

# LITERARY LIVERPOOL

Throughout Liverpool there are clusters of streets named after famous literary characters. Some famous writers are named more than once, while others are not featured at all. Some less well-known writers are present too. In many ways, it has all come down to the personal tastes of the developer, with the most recent builders still using literary figures when naming streets.

Joshua Rose, who owned a lot of land in the Scotland Road and Great Homer Street area at the turn of the 19th century, was the first developer to build streets in Liverpool with a literary theme. He named **Rose Hill, Rose Place** and **Rose Vale** after himself, but in the other streets he developed his interest in the arts, especially poetry, was evident. There was a road known as Sickmans Lane as it was where victims of the Bubonic Plague had been interred and buried in the 14th century. Rose then formally named this **Addison Street**, after Joseph Addison (1672-1719), a poet who regularly contributed to *The Tatler* and *The Spectator*. On the other side of Byrom Street streets were named after poets of an even earlier age. **Chaucer Street** was named after Geoffrey Chaucer, author of the 14th century *Canterbury Tales* and **Juvenal Street** commemorates a Roman satirical poet, Decimus Junius Juvenalis (65-128 AD). He painted a vivid description of Roman society with his satires. **Comus Street** is not written after a poet or author, but a play itself. *Comus*, a masque,[25] was written by John Milton and first presented in Ludlow in 1634, but developed further in the early 1800s.

By 1810, Rose had laid out **Great Homer Street** as a continuation of Fox Street, but it was not for another ten years that it was built upon and twenty before it extended further than Rose Vale. Homer was a Greek poet from c.850 BC who composed two epic poems in an impersonal style detailing events that happened many years before they were written. One of these poems, *The Iliad*, is remembered by **Iliad Street**. This poem dealt with events of the Trojan War, fought between the Greeks and the city of Troy in Turkey. Linking Great Homer Street with Iliad Street is **Sheridan Street**, named after Richard Brinsley Sheridan (1751-1816), a dramatist who managed the Drury Lane theatre in London and also served in Parliament as Under-Secretary for Foreign Affairs and Secretary to the Treasury.

---

[25] Form of dramatic writing containing music and dance. '

Soon after Great Homer Street, **Roscommon Street** was laid out by Rose and named after Wentworth Dillon, 4th Earl of Roscommon (1633-85). He formed a literary society with John Dryden (1631-1700), after whom **Dryden Street** is named. Dryden wrote many poems depicting historical figures, such as *Heroic Stanzas*, which commemorated Oliver Cromwell. At the Kirkdale Road end of Great Homer Street is **Medea Street**, named after the Greek tragedy play[26] *Medea*. The hero of this play, Jason, is commemorated by **Jason Street**, which runs off it. These streets have only been developed since the Second World War, continuing the theme of a number of Greek named streets that have disappeared such as Zante Street, Candia Street and Crete Street. These streets have now disappeared but **Mitylene Street**, named after a Greek island, still exists in a much shortened form off Netherfield Road North.

Sir Walter Scott (1771-1832) was a Scottish poet and novelist whose historical works created a great interest in Scottish traditions. His works are remembered especially in Aigburth, with **Marmion Road** being named after an 1808 poem of the same name and **Ivanhoe Road, Mannering Road** and **Waverley Road** being named after novels (*Ivanhoe, Guy Mannering and Waverley*). The principal character in *Guy Mannering* is Harry Bertram, commemorated in **Bertram Road**. Another character from one of Scott's poems is Lochinvar, who features in *Marmion*. He gives his name to **Lochinvar Street** in Walton, which is situated next to **Peveril Street**, named after Scott's novel *Peveril Peak*. In Everton, between St Anne Street and Shaw Street **Roderick Street, Rokeby Street** and **Rokeby Close** remember two more of Scott's poems. Elsewhere in Everton off Netherfield Road North, **Robsart Street** is named after Amy Robsart, a character from Scott's novel *Kenilworth*. This street was once named Tarleton Street, after the family of merchants who had a house there, but it was changed after Everton's absorption into Liverpool to avoid confusion. **Abbotsford Road** in Norris Green remembers the last home of Scott, Abbotsford House, on the banks of the Tweed in Melrose.

One of the reasons that Sir Walter Scott turned to novel writing from poetry was due to the popularity of Lord Byron (1788-1824), one of the most versatile of the romantic poets. He is remembered by **Byron Street**, off Banks Road in Garston, which is next to **Otway Street**,

---

[26] Play with an unhappy ending

named after dramatist Thomas Otway (1652-85) and **Shakespeare Street**, named after the world's most famous playwright William Shakespeare (1564-1616). Another street in this vicinity is **Marlowe Close**, which was inspired by Christopher Marlowe, who was stabbed to death in a tavern brawl in 1593, aged 29. His play *Edward II* was a model for Shakespeare's *Richard II* and *Richard III*. Also present is **Shelley Grove**, named after another romantic poet, Percy Bysshe Shelley (1792-1822).

For such a revered playwright, William Shakespeare is not as widely remembered in Liverpool as might be expected. In addition to being commemorated in Garston, there is a **Shakespeare Close** in Everton while **Verona Street** in Anfield commemorates one of his plays, *The Two Gentlemen of Verona*. The only cluster of streets is in the Bank Hall area. **Celia Street** and **Rosalind Way** are named after characters from *As you Like It*, while a character named Beatrice appears in both this play and *Twelfth Night* and gives her name to **Beatrice Street**. *Henry V* characters gave their names to **Falstaff Street** and **Hotspur Street** with **Oberon Street, Miranda Place** and **Portia Street** being named after characters from *A Midsummer Nights Dream*, *The Tempest* and *The Merchant of Venice* respectively. **Hector Place** is named after a character from *Troilus and Cressida*, while **Macbeth Street** and **Othello Close** remember titles of Shakespeare's plays. There are more Shakespeare themed streets over the Liverpool/Sefton boundary in Bootle.

In Toxteth, between North Hill Street and Upper Warwick Street, the work of Charles Dickens (1812-70), whose novels provided an acute social commentary of the time, have been heavily remembered. Several of these original streets have been demolished and rebuilt as closes. Amongst those present are **Barkis Close** and **Micawber Close**, named after characters in Dickens's novel *David Copperfield*. There is also a **Copperfield Close** itself and the novels of *Little Dorrit*, *Dombey and Son and Nicholas Nickleby* are all remembered by **Dorrit Street, Dombey Street,** and **Nickleby Close**. These are in addition to a **Dickens Street**, which needs no explanation, as well as **Pecksniff Street**, named after a character from *Martin Chuzzlewitt*. One of Dickens first works was the *Pickwick Papers*, published in monthly instalments between 1836 and 1837. **Tupman Street, Weller Street** and **Winkle Street** are named after characters from this, while the novel itself is remembered by **Pickwick Street**.

As well as being well represented in Toxteth, Dickens has another cluster of streets named after his novels on an estate between Earle Road and Tunnel Road in Edge Hill. This was re-developed in the early 1980s, with the new closes retaining the names of the old terraced streets that disappeared. Noah Claypole, a character from *Oliver Twist* gives his name to **Claypole Close**, but characters from the novel *Our Mutual Friend* influence the other Dickens streets. These are **Lightwood Drive** (Mortimer Lightwood), **Rokesmith Avenue** (John Rokesmith), **Wilfer Close** (Bella Wilfer) and **Wrayburn Close** (Eugene Wrayburn).

Near to these Dickens streets, some American poets of the Victorian era have been honoured off Smithdown Road. Oliver Wendell Holmes (1809-94), a writer of witty verse is remembered by **Wendell Street** and **Holmes Street**, while John Greenleaf Whittier (1807-92) gives his name to **Greenleaf Street** and **Whittier Street**. **Cullen Street** commemorates William Cullen Bryant (1794-1878). **Longfellow Street**, which runs across the top of all five of these streets, is named after Henry Wadsworth Longfellow (1807-82), the first American to have a bust made in his honour in Poets Corner in Westminster Abbey. A less well-known American poet, Henry Vandyke (1852-1933) is remembered by **Vandyke Street**. Parallel to Longfellow Street, the theme turns to British writers with **Boswell Street** being named after James Boswell (1740-95), a friend and biographer to poet Samuel Johnson. **Wordsworth Street** commemorates William Wordsworth (1770-1850), one of the most influential of the Romantic poets.

Herman Melville, best remembered for *Moby Dick*, wrote the semi-autobiographical novel *Redburn* in 1849, which describes his experiences in Liverpool as a cabin boy. **Melville Street** in Toxteth is not actually named after him but when surrounding streets were demolished the opportunity was taken to name a new street off it **Redburn Close**.

One of the great Victorian poets was Lord Alfred Tennyson (1809-92). He was the first poet to be made a peer of the realm and had produced several blank verse plays and an epic by the age of fifteen. In 1842 he published the two volume *Poems*, which included *Morte d'Arthur*, an idyll based on the Arthurian legend, which is a group of middle aged tales about the legendary Arthur, King of the Britons. His second Arthurian work, *Idylls of the King*, was written between 1859 and 1885 and these tales are remembered between North Hill Street and Upper Warwick Street in Toxteth. **Merlin Street** is named after a counsellor of King Arthur and **Modred Street** after his nephew, with **Elaine Street, Enid Street, Geraint Street** and **Gwendoline Street** also being named after people from the legend. **Celtic Street** takes its name from the Celtic origins of the Arthurian legend, while **Maud Street** is named after one of Tennyson's other works, *Maud and Other Poems*. Tennyson himself was commemorated by Tennyson Street, which was later replaced by Tennyson Walk, although this has been lost to redevelopment in recent years.

Amongst other streets in Toxteth lost to recent redevelopment are Makepeace Walk and Thackeray Close, Place and Street, which were situated on the Carter-Thackeray estate. These were named after William Makepeace Thackeray, who was the author of realistic novels that emphasised social systems and made him a rival to Charles Dickens. Near to the junction of Breck Road and Belmont Road in Anfield there are three streets named after his novels, **Esmond Street** (*Henry Esmond*), **Pendennis Street** (*Pendennis*) and **Newcombe Street** (*The Newcombes*). There is also a **Becky Street**, named after Becky Sharp, a character from *Vanity Fair*. Alongside this group of streets is **Sedley Street**, which although not linked to Thackeray, does have literary connections. Sir Charles Sedley (1639-1701) was an English dramatist and poet whose comedy plays include *Bellamira* and *The Mulberry Garden*.

Benjamin Disraeli, who was Prime Minister in 1868 and 1874-80, also pursued a writing career. He has five streets in Anfield named after his novels; **Lothair Road, Alroy Road, Sybil Road, Coningsby Road** and **Tancred Road**.

The development of Edge Hill had gathered pace by the 1860s as merchants' villas became swamped by terraced housing, with some of the main streets of the old settlement being re-named. Lord Street was divided into two and named **Overbury Street**, after poet Sir Thomas Overbury (1581-1613) and **Overton Street**, after leader of the Leveller[27] movement Richard Overton, who wrote *Mans Morality* in 1643. King Street was re-named **Kinglake Street**, after Alexander William Kinglake (1809-91), who in 1844 wrote *Eothen: or Traces of Travel Brought home From the East.* This was an account of travels ten years earlier and he also wrote a history of the Crimean War. Other Edge Hill Streets named after literary figures are **Shenstone Street** and **Sidney Place**. The former was named after poet and essayist William Shenstone (1714-63), writer of T*he Schoolmistress* and *The Judgement of Hercules*, while the latter takes its name from Sir Philip Sidney (1554-86). He was a courtier to Queen Elizabeth I and his poetry was published posthumously following his premature death from a musket wound suffered during a skirmish with some Spanish soldiers.

In the late 1990s new development has occurred on the site of a former school off Childwall Valley Road and Chelwood Avenue. This has led to some 20th century literary figures being remembered. **Baldwin Avenue** is named after Stanley Baldwin, who was Prime Minister from 1923-4 and 1935-7. He later became a writer and his books include *Classics* and the *Plain Man and Peace and Goodwill.* John Masefield, who was poet laureate 1930-67, spent his sea cadetship on Merseyside and the anchor of his training ship, HMS Conway stands outside the Merseyside Maritime Museum entrance. He published a book of poems, *Sea Water Ballads* in 1902. He has written more poems commemorating events on Merseyside than any other poet and is remembered by **Masefield Grove**. Another poet laureate, from 1972-84, was John Betjeman who also wrote a number of books about architecture. He gives his name to **Betjeman Grove** while **Swinburne Close** is named after Algernon Charles Swinburne (1837-1909), whose *Poems and Ballads* in 1866 caused a famous Victorian literary scandal due to its sexual content.

---

[27] 17th Century political group active during the English Civil War.

# SPEKE AND OTHER LOCAL AUTHORITY DEVELOPMENTS

In the inter war years large scale development by Liverpool Corporation took pace in outlying districts of the city in order to house people from the slums of the inner-city.

Generally speaking, most of the streets were named after towns, which gave a virtually unending supply of names to choose from. However, there were some exceptions, most notably in Speke, while the Militant Tendency had some novel names for streets when they built new houses in the 1980s.

For centuries Speke was no more than a scattered group of cottages and a collection of farms that were inter-linked by lanes. It had a population of no more than 400, but this changed in 1921 following the death of Adelaide Watt, the last owner of Speke Hall. The house itself was taken over by the National Trust, but the majority of the estate was bought by Liverpool Corporation and earmarked for a development to house people being moved from the inner city. The aim was to build a satellite town that would be a countrywide model, ending social segregation by providing accommodation and amenities side by side for all sections of the community. Some of the old lanes remained, with a lot of new roads being named after local landmarks and woodland.

The most famous owners of Speke Hall had been the Norris family, who were lords of the manor for nearly 400 years until the mid 18th century. Surprisingly, no streets are named directly after them, but an estate that belonged to them at Blackrod, near Bolton, gives its name to **Blackrod Avenue**. One of the earlier lords of the manor, Benedict de Gerneth is commemorated in **Gerneth Road** and **Gerneth Close**. He had taken over the land not long after the Domesday survey of 1086 and one of his descendants, Roger de Gerneth was Speke's chief forester[28] in the 12th century. In ancient times challenge fights used to take place between the villages of Hale, Halewood and Speke. These took place on a piece of land at the boundary of all three, named the Conleach, which gives its name to **Conleach Road**.

**Speke Town Lane** is one of the original lanes of the estate, although it is now considerably shorter than it was. This led to Speke Town Farm,

---

[28] Official appointed by the King to adminster the Forest Law.

which stood near the junction of Speke Boulevard and Speke Hall Road. Another lane to be shortened was **Woodend Lane**, which led to Woodend Farm on the site of the 'Evans' factory. Presumably, the farm was named as it was at the end of a wood. Some of the first corporation houses to be built were on **Hale Road**, which already existed leading to the village of Hale. All Saints Church, which had been built in 1876 gave its name to **All Saints Road** and **Speke Church Road**, the latter of which was part of a longer lane called Hall Lane that led all the way to Speke Hall. **School Way** takes its name from the original sandstone village school, which was replaced by the much larger Stockton Wood Comprehensive in 1940. Built around the time of the church, the old school building is still in use today as the church hall.

Obvious examples of farms that had to make way for the estate and been remembered in street names are **Goldfinch Farm Road** and **Greyhound Farm Road**. The latter was also the local pub until Adelaide Watt took its licence away and its last owners are remembered by **Critchley Road**. Other farms remembered are **Blacklock Hall Road, Tewit Hall Road, Tewit Hall Close,** and **Sutton Wood Road**, named after the farm of Sutton Grange that stood on the site of the old airport runway.

A farm still in existence is Linner Farm, on Halebank Road. This gave its name to **Linner Road** and probably derives from the 14th century park of Linnall in Hale. Ramsbrook Farm is also in existence in Halebank, taking its name from the Rams Brook, a stream that once flowed right through the present day estate. In addition to the farm, the stream has also given its name to **Ramsbrook Road** and **Ramsbrook Close**. Another farm between Speke and Hale is Heath Gate Farm, after which **Heathgate Avenue** is named.

Speke Hall is very well known locally, but a smaller hall that is remembered is Lovel's Hall, after which **Lovel Road** and **Lovel Way** are named. This was situated close to the junction of the M57 link road and Speke-Widnes road and was named by John Lovel who acquired it through marriage in the late 14th century. The builders of the hall were the Holland family, who are commemorated by **Holland Road**, off Damwood Road. The hall came into the hands of the Earls of Derby after the 15th century Wars of the Roses and although long since disappeared, its outline and filled-in moat can still be seen from the air. As well as local farms and buildings being commemorated, a number of woodland areas also have streets in Speke named after them, many of which are still in existence. **Damwood Road** and **East Damwood Road** take their name from the Dam Wood, which was situated on the site of the airport runway. Stockton's Wood and The Clough are two remaining pieces of woodland in the grounds of Speke Hall and they give their names to **Clough Road** and **Stockton Wood Road**. Even nearer to the built up area of Speke is Little Heath Wood, on the corner of Dungeon Lane and Hale Road. **Little Heath Road** is named after this.

Over the county boundary in the Cheshire borough of Halton are Mill Wood and the Clamley Park plantation. These give their names to **Millwood Road, East Millwood Road** and **Clamley Road**. Further afield, on the northern fringe of Hough Green is the Alder Wood, from which **Alderwood Avenue** is named. Harefield, a piece of land that gives its name to **Harefield Road** and **Harefield Green**, lies off Lower Road. Presumably this name simply comes from a field that hares inhabited. **Leveret Road**, off East Millwood Road, takes its name from the leveret, which is a small hare.

Although local history influenced many of the street names in Speke, as time went on the newer streets were named less imaginatively. Main roads east of Western Avenue were laid out on a grid pattern, with **Western Avenue** forming the gateway to the estate from Speke Boulevard and **Central Way** and **Central Avenue** leading away in opposite directions from the shopping area. Old Hutte Lane was re-named **Eastern Avenue** and the western/eastern theme continued with the relatively minor **Northern Road** and **Southern Road**. The roads circling the pedestrian precinct were mundanely named **North Parade** and **South Parade**. Many of the greens and closes, which were built off the main roads, were named after towns and villages. **Ardwick Road, Burnage Close, Heaton Close** and **Withington Road** were all named after districts of Manchester, while Wirral places have given their names to **Prenton Green, Upton Close** and **Upton Green**.

Work on the Norris Green estate started in 1926 and a large number of the streets are named after places in Cumbria. Examples include **Scargreen Avenue** and **Stainburn Avenue**, which are named after places, and **Bowscale Road** and **Branstree Avenue**, which take their names from fells. In Dovecot, where building started in 1930, places from different corners of the country are remembered. **Ancroft Road, Colwell Road, Croxdale Road** and **Gainford Road** take their names from northeast towns and villages, while **Broadoak Road, Chedworth Road, Somerford Road** and **Winstone Road** are named after places in Gloucestershire. **Grovehurst Avenue, Kemsley Road, Lunsford Road** and **Lynsted Road** represent Kent place names

Streets named after place names are repeated in other corporation developments around the city, but during the 1980s some different names were used. The left wing city council, led by John Hamilton and Derek Hatton embarked on a major house-building programme under the Urban Re-generation Strategy. The slum clearance saw a lot of street names disappear altogether and several more re-named as closes or ways. In addition to this, a number of whole new names were introduced reflecting the council's socialist tendencies at the time.

Although **St Joseph's Crescent**, off Christian Street, was named after a local church, it is co-incidentally apt that St. Joseph is the patron saint of workers. His feast day is 1st May and was selected as a counter celebration to the Soviet Union's May Day celebrations. Also off Christian Street is **Tom Mann Close**, named after the co-founder of the Workers Union, which eventually merged with others to form the TGWU.[29] In 1911 he led the transport workers strike in Liverpool and consequently served six months in jail for sedition. In Vauxhall, **Tolpuddle Way** is named after the Tolpuddle Martyrs, six farm labourers who were sentenced to transportation to Australia in 1834 after asking for a rise in wages. After a public outrage they were pardoned two years later and their struggle was a landmark in trade union history, with the right to 'free collective bargaining' being established.

Also in Vauxhall, two Irish political activists are commemorated. Back Bond Street disappeared and **O'Connell Road** was developed, named after early 19th century Irish political rights leader Daniel O'Connell. Another Irish Nationalist, James Larkin is commemorated by **James Larkin Way** in Kirkdale. He played a part in the 1916 Easter Rebellion. Next to James Larkin Way is **Sharpeville Close**, which commemorates

---

[29] Trade and General Workers Union.

85

the Sharpeville massacre of 1960 when sixty people were killed as South African police opened fire on a crowd of Black protesters.

Three new streets off Upper Stanhope Street in Toxteth reflect Liverpool's support for Nicaragua's left wing Sandinista government during this period. **Corinto Street** is named after the country's Pacific port with which very close ties were developed, while **Bluefields Street** is named after a Nicaraguan port on the Caribbean coast. **Sandino Street** commemorates Augusto Cesar Sandino, the 1920s guerrilla leader from whom the rebel group took its name when it was formed in the 1960s.

# 20TH CENTURY PRIVATE DEVELOPMENTS

While many streets developed by the council were often named after places, private developers have sometimes been more imaginative in the naming of streets in Liverpool. However, when stuck, they have often reverted to the more simple method too.

In Stoneycroft, classical architectural styles were remembered in the 1920s. **Doric Road, Ionic Road** and **Corinthian Avenue** are named after the three different types of Greek architectural column, while their decorative features are remembered by **Abacus Road** and **Acanthus Road**. The Etruscan civilisation, who lived on the Italian peninsula before the Roman Empire have given their name to **Etruscan Road**, while **Podium Road** takes its name from the base on which Etruscan temples would stand. **Classic Road** is named after the classical forms of architecture, which the Greeks and Romans adapted. This was revived in the Renaissance of the 15th and 16th centuries by Italian architects including Andrea Palladio, who has been commemorated in **Palladio Road**. **Florentine Road** remembers the architects of Florence who contributed to this renaissance, while **Inigo Road** is named after Inigo Jones, an English architect of the 17th century who was inspired by Palladio.

Liverpool's famous river is the Mersey, but its little sister, the Alt, has not been forgotten. In Croxteth Park, perhaps the city's most famous street, **Brookside**, takes its name from its proximity to the rivers. On the same estate there is a **Riverside**, while river features give their names to **Delta Drive, Oxbow Road** and **The Meander**. Another water feature, now disused is the Kensington Reservoir. This has given its name to a very recent development, **Clearwater Close**.

For a city so steeped in football heritage, the sport is virtually forgotten about in the local street names and is only commemorated in two places. **Mere Green** in Walton takes its name from the original name for Everton FC's Goodison Park ground. **Bob Paisley Court**, a sheltered block, is situated barely a goal kick away from the Kop end at Anfield and remembers Liverpool FC managerial legend Bob Paisley.

Liverpool's famous horse race, the Grand National is well represented by local street names, with an estate bordering Aintree racecourse along its lines. Streets present include **Red Rum Close**, named after the three times 1970s winner, while **Eremon Close, Sunloch Close, Sprig Close, Kilmore Close** and **Anglo Close** are named after the winners of 1907, 1914, 1927, 1962 and 1966. Other streets on this estate linked to the race are **Seagram Close**, after a former sponsor, **Furlong Close**, named after a horse racing term of distance and **Steeplechase Close**, referring to the fact the Grand National is run over jumps. In nearby Warbreck Park, **Woodbrook Avenue, Foinavon Close, Sundew Close, Lucius Close** and **Ayala Close** are all named after past winners of the race.

A number of famous golf courses give their names to streets locally too. Off Yew Tree Lane in West Derby, opposite the golf course are a number of streets named after other courses. The main road on the estate is **St. Andrews Avenue**, named after the famous Scottish course, which was the venue for the 2000 Open. Other Scottish courses are commemorated in **Carnoustie Close, Muirfield Close, Troon Close** and **Turnberry Close**, while **Belfry Close, Fulford Close, Rye Grove** and **Lytham Close** are named after English courses. Off Townsend Lane, **Birkdale Close** was built around the time of the 1984 Open, which was held at Birkdale, near Southport.

This is not to say private developers have not resorted to place names too however. An example is off Childwall Valley Road, where a number of towns and villages in the south-west are honoured. Examples are **Okehampton Road, Padstow Road** and **Paignton Road**. Not too far away off Childwall Park Avenue the south-west is honoured again, with **Devon Gardens, Woolacombe Road** and **Churston Road**.

Living things have been a common example of how streets are named, especially from the 1970s. In Walton **Freesia Avenue** and **Honeysuckle Drive** are some of a large number of streets named after plants. In Croxteth Park a number of birds are commemorated, with **Chaffinch Close** and **Lapwing View** amongst those present. Also in this area are some streets named after types of fish, including **Grayling Drive** and **Zander Grove**.

How streets will be named in the future remains to be seen, but one development at the end of the 1990s off East Prescot Road did have an astrological theme. The estate comprises **Taurus Road, Aquarius Close, Capricorn Crescent, Leo Close, Aries Close, Scorpio Close** and **Libra Close**.

Liverpool's most famous sons are the Beatles. In the 1980s **George Harrison Close, John Lennon Drive, Paul McCartney Way** and **Ringo Starr Drive** were all named after them in Kensington. It has recently been proposed that North John Street be renamed John Street, or even John Lennon Street, a topic that sparked fierce debate. The naming of streets in Liverpool looks like it will continue to generate interest for many years to come.

# INDEX